THE WOODWORKING BIBLE

The ultimate guide to master all the major woodworking techniques | Includes easy and affordable indoor & outdoor projects with step-by-step blueprints

3 IN 1

By

MIKE WILLIAMS

Table Of Contents

INTRODUCTION 6

BOOK 1: TECHNIQUES... 8

INTRODUCTION 9
CHAPTER 1: LEARN THE BASICS OF WOOD WORK............ 11
CHAPTER 2: WOOD SELECTION....................................... 14
   The Softwoods 15
   The Hardwoods 16
   Choosing the Right Wood 19
CHAPTER 3: WOODWORKING TECHNIQUES.................... 22
   Woodworking Techniques..23
   Four Processes Involved in Wood Processing 31
   Advantages and Disadvantages 35
   Types of Sawing 37
CHAPTER 4: TYPES OF JOINTS IN WOODWORK PROJECTS 39
   How to Fasten Joning Pieces in Woodwork 41
CONCLUSION... 43

BOOK 2: TOOLS 44

INTRODUCTION 45
CHAPTER 1: WOODWORKING TOOLS.............................. 48
   The Claw Hammer 48
   The Tape Measure 49
   The Utility Knife..49
   The Moisture Meter 49
   The Chisel 50
   The Level 51
   The Screwdriver 51
   The Nail Set..51

The Sliding Bevel 51

The Layout Square 52

The Hand Plane 52

The Caliper 53

The Clamp 53

The Jig Jig 54

The Hand Saw 54

The Feather Board 55

The Metal Detector 55

CHAPTER 2: CATEGORIZATION OF WOODWORKING TOOLS 56

CHAPTER 3: TYPES OF HAND TOOLS 59

CHAPTER 4: ASSEMBLAGE TOOLS 63

The Power Drills 63

The Screw Guns 63

The Hammers 64

The Mallets 64

CHAPTER 5: SHARPENING TOOLS 65

CHAPTER 6: TIPS AND TRICKS FOR WOODWORKING 67

Wood Layout Triangle 68

Story Stick 68

Drill Depth 68

Glue Cleanup 68

Wax Paper Cover 69

Hold Glue-Ups Instantly 69

Sandpaper Organization 69

CHAPTER 7: COMMON WOODWORKING MISTAKES AND HOW TO AVOID THEM 70

A Table that Rocks 70

Wood that Splits When Being Cut 70

Joints that are Too Loose 71

CONCLUSION 72

BOOK 3: PROJECTS 73

INTRODUCTION **74**

CHAPTER 1: BASIC WOOD WORK PROJECTS **76**

CHAPTER 2: CHOOSING WHAT TO CONSTRUCT **80**

CHAPTER 3: WOODWORKING PROJECTS **83**

Home Furnishing 83

Home Accessories 94

Outdoor Accessories 105

CHAPTER 4: MISTAKES AND HOW TO AVOID THEM **129**

CONCLUSION **134**

CONCLUSION **135**

INTRODUCTION

Woodworking is more complex than it seems at first from rustic green wood carving to detail and accurate cabinet-making. Furniture making is the name assigned to this practice by most citizens, although in industry this applies mainly to the design of house-building structural woodwork, which is typically completed on site. A skilled woodworker understands how to make the best of different products, from natural timber to fiberglass or strand boarding. It's not only about machine ability but architecture and preparation as well.

Wood is such a workable stuff; it must have been one of the first items that humanity used to build structures and devices for the simplest of instruments. There's a wide variety of tree varieties that come in varying grades and have to be dried to avoid movement until it's sorted out for most traditional jobs. For starters, there are several different professional woodworkers; woodcarvers barrel makers, chair makers, wheelwrights, shipwrights, and instrument manufacturers.

Woodworking often includes a broad variety of functionality a piece of work may be kept together with only nails or intricately made joints; wooden frameworks in houses are typically held together with screws and nails , although a chair or an older house can have mortia and tenon joints. In various situations, skilled woodworkers utilize a number of specific joints to withstand the various stresses imposed on the finished product. Definitions of joints cover miters, bridles, feet, plates, housings, dovetails, buttocks, tongues & groove, mortices & tenons, half or lap joints.

There are times where utilizing other man-made items such as plywood makes sense – creating box-type buildings such as wardrobes, kitchens, and other cabinetry is much more economical. In that case utilizing solid wood is a bit of a mistake.

To develop expertise and the belief that you know the best way to handle a task, attend a woodworking course. While the word "woodworker" can invoke the picture of an artist who uses hand tools to create ornate furniture, the modern woodworking trade is highly technological and depends on specialized machinery and highly skilled operators. For perform most of the job, employees utilize electronic equipment, such as computerized numerical control (CNC) devices. Most of the research is performed in a high-volume assembly line plant, although there is still some specialized research that does not lend itself to assembly line manufacturing.

BOOK 1: TECHNIQUES

Introduction

The woodwork technique is one of the most important modules a wood carving artist must undergo.

It takes you on a tour of learning basic design elements in the art of wood carving. It teaches you the importance of choosing the right wood for your project and then proceeding with it. It also introduces you to the crafting process by giving you step-by-step guidelines to follow, from the wood cutting to finishing the object.

The main focus of this module is to enhance the user's imagination and creativity, believing that drawing is not a difficult task anyone can do, but it's a talent. The module demonstrates some more advanced techniques and objects to try out. It then provides you with a list of things to avoid in your art objects by reminding you of the secrets you need to keep to become a good carver.

This module's main purpose is to teach woodcarving techniques and guide you to apply them in your own woodwork tasks. Without following the guide provided here, you may find yourself being unsuccessful and not getting what you want, even with lots of energy and effort. True success lies in learning the right techniques, carving objects that your mind rather than your hands want to create and displaying them in front of people who are our audience.

What you will learn

Looking after wood: You will learn everything you need to know, including the different types of wood available and their basic usage.

Design: You will learn the importance of good design and how to translate this idea into your own concepts.

Now that you know what you need to do ask yourself what you would like to achieve with your wooden objects and how. Regretfully, you will never become a legendary carver by starting off without understanding the basic nature of wood and its properties. Think of a writing expert; his pen is his medium.

So, let's start!

Chapter 1:
Learn the Basics of Wood Work

Starting with woodworking, you need to keep in mind some of the aspects to avail the most of it. This art also hold some basics which if followed can help you go through this art easily and if not you can suffer.

Safety rules: Every work when done without taking precaution can be dangerous. Woodworking is easy and fun, but it should be dealt with great precautions. Always wear safety equipment which includes safety gloves (latex gloves), hearing protection aid, and safety glasses and face mask

Clothing: Always wear proper clothes but make sure they should not be loose as they can interfere with the work you will be doing. Wear long sleeves shirt and long pants with good steel toed work shoes for comfortable working. An apron is also necessary for working with particular machines.

Organize tools: The very tricky work to be done during woodworking is an organization of the tools. The tools need to be kept safe so they can be found when necessary and work smoothly for years to come. Small objects like nails, things for writing should be kept in separate boxes. Tools should be oiled when needed with proper protection covering for their optimum performance.

Disconnect electricity before changing blade from any tool: Whenever you feel the need to change the blade from any power tool make sure you switched off the electricity as it is a dangerous practice and can cause you to lose your finger/s.

Sharp blades: The sharpness of the blade is very necessary. If the blade is not sharp, it will result in spending of a lot of energy on one task and the blade will bend. The cut produced will not be sharp as well.

Removing of waste material: Whenever working with a power tool never put your hands near the blade especially when you are trying to remove the waste. Wait until the blade has completely stopped and try to use a scrap cloth or any stick to remove the waste.

Do not get distracted: Always focus on the work. Every work comes with a set of distractions, but it is the responsibility of the worker to avoid these distractions and work with full concentration. If you encounter any distraction make sure to complete your work first and switch off any power tool and then put your focus towards the distraction.

Stock of items: Always keep a good stock of nails, screws, wood and other material so that you do not actually have to run at the eleventh hour. If you lose the stock of any of this item, you have to stop your complete project in the middle and wait for the things to come.

Selection of wood:

- For the selection of the wood the first thing needed is to take a look at the defects from all four sides. Multiple factors can contribute to the defects in the log of the tree which can be caused by improper drying or milling techniques, fungus, knots, insects, lightning strikes and improper growth pattern. But remember not all the defects can be the reason to reject a piece of log. These defects can be used as the exquisite design for the woodwork.

- All you need is to take the piece of wood you wish to examine over the ground and look it at the level of your eye and look for any bowing. Examine from four corners of the block.

- Look for the twist with the same technique as for bow.

- Look for crook as which is usually caused by overgrown parts of the bark.

- Look for cracks. They are formed by separation of fibres due to drying. Checks occur when the wood is wet and can become larger when the wood gets dried.

Making hole: One mistake that the beginner usually make is with the making of a hole in the wood. When a number of screw or nail is driven close to one another, they result in tearing up of the block. To avoid this hole should be made less than the fixing nail or screw so it will prevent splitting.

Marking on the wood: Marking on the woods to decide to where to cut are very necessary. Use pencils to mark the areas you need to cut. Use a scale or measuring tape for accurate measurements. For long lines, use the scale for perfect lines. Use arrow head for indicating the direction of the cut.

Chapter 2:
Wood Selection

However, of all the different kinds, there are several that are most preferred by woodworkers for their quality and looks. The different kinds of wood are classified as either softwoods or hardwoods, with each having features that are sought after for particular kinds of projects

The Softwoods

1. Cedar

Of all the varieties of cedar present in the country, the western red cedar is the one most commonly employed in woodwork. As the name implies, the western red has a reddish color in its wood. It also has a straight grain and a slightly aromatic smell, which many people like. The western red cedar is one of the softer woods and rates at 1 in 4 on the wood hardness scale. However, its high resistance to9 rotting makes it favorable for use in building products intended for outdoor use, such as garden furniture, decks, and building extensions.

2. Pine

The pine tree is one of the most common species of softwood trees in America, with several popular varieties like the Ponderosa, sugar, white, and yellow pines. As it is also relatively soft and lightweight, pine is easy to work with, making it a popular choice for indoor furniture, as well as carving and is especially favored by woodworkers from the south-western regions. The pine has a pale yellow to light brown hue.

3. Fir

A slice of wood from the Douglas fir

One of the most prominent features of the fir is the grain, which pronounced and straight, and with a reddish tint. However, it isn't as interesting to look at compared to other wood grain, which is why most woodworkers opt to use it for pieces they intend to paint. Another valuable feature of the fir (specifically of the Douglas fir) is its strength and hardness, which is relatively high for softwood, which is why it is heavily used in construction. As it is relatively inexpensive, woodworkers also choose it for the above qualities.

4. Redwood

Redwood timber

Redwood is mostly used for outdoor projects mainly due to its high moisture resistance, which is similar to cedar. As is with other softwoods, it is relatively easy to work with. The Redwood also has a beautiful reddish tint to its grain, which why it is favored as a decorative material. It is also inexpensive and can be readily bought from any local home center.

The Hardwoods

1. Ash

Slice of European ash

Of the popular types of hardwood, ash is one of the easiest to work with, having a hardness of 4. This, combined with its strength, makes it suitable for use in making high strength sports equipment like baseball bats and hockey sticks, as well as boat parts and tool handles. However, ash has become harder to acquire these days, and can only be procured through large lumber yards, which is why they are a bit expensive than other woods.

2. Birch

Silver birch wood

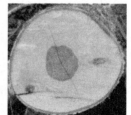

One of the best things about birch is that it is relatively inexpensive and is relatively easy to find, being available in most home centers. It is also relatively strong, with a hardness of 4. There are two different varieties of birch commonly preferred by woodworkers: yellow and white. Yellow birch has a pale yellow to white color with a reddish tint in its hardwood. On the other hand, white birch looks a bit similar to a maple.

3. Cherry

Cherry wood

Cherry is well known as being one of the easiest to stain woods, which also brings out the natural beauty of its reddish brown heartwood. Also, it is relatively soft, with a hardness of 2, and is easy to work with, making it ideal for building furniture. However, as it is highly in demand, procuring it might be a bit harder than other woods, which also makes it a bit more expensive.

4. Mahogany

Mahogany is one of the most well-known of the furniture woods. It is highly favored both for its hardness, with a rating 2, and its natural beauty coming from its deep red tint, medium texture, and straight grain. This can be further enhanced by staining, which mahogany takes in easily. Aside from being used for fine furniture, mahogany is also often employed in boatbuilding and crafting decorative pieces.

5. Maple

Bench made from maple

There are two varieties of maple commonly used in woodworking: hard and soft. However, despite the names, both are actually harder than most other woods, with hard maple topping it at 5 in the hardness scale, making it difficult to work with. Soft maple, though, is easier to use. However, both are more stable than other woods, making them desirable for use in outdoor applications.

6. Oak

White oak tree

Yet another popular choice for making furniture, the oak comes in two different varieties: red and white. White oak is more often chosen for its beauty, as well as its resistance to moisture, which makes it ideal for outdoor pieces like boat parts. However, both are well known for their strength and hardness (with a hardness of 4).

7. Poplar

Furniture made from poplar

Aside from being very easy to work with (it has a hardness of just 1), poplar is also one of the least expensive woods. It is not as commonly used in fine furniture as other wood varieties that have more beautiful grain, and in the rare cases that it is it; is almost always painted over. Nevertheless, it is still preferred for making cabinet drawers, because of its strength and durability, as well as cost.

8. Teak

Close-up of a teak table

Teak is well-known for its high weather resistance, which makes it a good choice for outdoor furniture and products. The golden brown color of its wood is another attraction. However, as it is of a high demand, teak has become a lot harder to get these days, raising the price a lot, often as much as $24 a foot. The wood is also moderately hard, placing in at 3 in the scale.

9. Walnut

Aside from furniture, walnut has also found a variety of other uses, including for carving and making gunstocks, mainly due to its moderate hardness (around 4 in the scale) and relative ease to work. The intricate grain and mix of coloration from light, grayish brown to purplish brown makes an attractive choice for decorative inlays. However, the wood it on the expensive side with boards costing around $8 a foot.

Choosing the Right Wood

Now that you are familiar with the kinds of wood available to you, it's time to know how to pick the right one in the lumberyard to suit your project. Here, you have some important points to take into consideration.

1. Type of project

As have been pointed above, different kinds of wood are preferred for different kinds of project. For instance, if you are planning to build a simple, unadorned side table, most inexpensive woods will suffice, while if you are going for something a bit more stylized, a higher quality wood will bring out the beauty of the design more. Fortunately, this is easy for beginners, as most projects provide exact specifications.

2. Type of wood

Often, there are several types of wood that can be used for a particular project, which might confuse a beginner as to what to pick. A useful point here is to determine which of the different wood types are more common in your area, as procuring them will be a lot easier. Also, note that there are some instances where softwoods can actually be substituted for hardwoods, as both have similar strengths. However, it would still be best for the beginner to refer to the specifications to determine the best-suited wood type.

3. Wood Grade

With the specific type of wood chosen, you can now consider wood grade. Wood are commonly graded as follows: No. 3B Common, No. 3A Common, Sound Wormy, No. 2B Common, No. 2A Common, No. 1 Common, Selects, FAS 1-Face FIF, and FAS, with FAS being the highest rating and is reserved for the finest projects. Wood grade is usually marked on the specifics of the sample provided in home centers and lumberyards.

4. Wood Condition

In some cases, a wood plank might look good from afar, but once you get working on it, a lot of imperfections show up. For instance, you might not be able to readily ascertain the straightness of a wood board at a first glance. Thus, it is a must to thoroughly inspect all the pieces of wood you purchase for a project to be sure they are free from defects. However, also note that there are instances where you can work around these defects, such as if the piece has to be cut and you can simply trim off the affected area. The next section lists some of the common wood defects you will encounter and ways of dealing with these.

5. Wood Price

Wood cost can be quite tricky for beginners who are not familiar with how this is assessed. Note that luxury woods are harder to acquire and as such, are more expensive. To save on costs, assess which parts of the project would need such high-end wood, and which sections can be done with a less expensive alternative. Also consider the type of finish you will do for the project. Get quotations from different sellers to have a better comparison of prices.

Defects;

bow crook kink cup twist

1. Bow

A bow is warping of the wood from one end to another.

2. Cup

A cup has the wood bending across the one of the faces.

3. Crook

A crook happens when the wood is warped along its edge.

4. Twist

A twist is severe bending of the wood, where the whole or part of the wood is warped in a screw-like manner.

5. Wood Knot

A not is an imperfection where the grain part around a circular discolored area. A knothole is a hole where the grain similarly parts around.

6. Split

A split is a crack in the wood, usually running from one end to another.

7. Check

A check is a crack running along the annular growth rings of the wood, but not through its entire thickness.

8. Wane

Waning happens when there is either some missing wood or bark still on the edges of the board.

Chapter 3:
Woodworking Techniques

When you're constructing a wooden object, it's important to understand the steps of the woodworking process. The process begins with sketching out the general direction of the project. The next step is defining the materials that you will need. Usually, woodworking projects are made of a combination of wood and other materials. For example, if your project is crafted from solid wood and veneer over a substrate, you will need different tools than if you are working with a solid piece of wood.

Using a pattern is another important aspect of simple design. This technique will help you make something that has visual appeal.

Woodworking Techniques

Measuring

The use of measuring instruments is essential for achieving a high-quality woodworking project. There are several types of measuring devices, including steel bench rulers, tape measures, and wood folding rulers. The most common general-marking tool is a 2H pencil, which has a medium-hard lead and leaves a fine line on most surfaces. Doing so will prevent inaccurate centered pencil points.

When measuring for woodworking projects, using a digital measuring device is a great option. These tools can do everything that analog measuring devices could, but they're far more accurate. Using a digital measuring instrument will increase your chances of obtaining accurate measurements and add consistency to your work. For best results, it's essential to follow a manufacturer's recommendations when purchasing woodworking measuring tools.

Another method for measuring is using a crow's foot. This method is useful when you're measuring a narrow board because you can mark a specific spot without using a ruler. For example, if a board is 8-5/32" wide, you must divide it into three equal widths. This method is simple enough that you can do it without a calculator.

Most craftsmen use a 12-foot tape measure. There's no other measuring instrument that's more used in woodworking. Most tape measures graduate in 1/16-inch increments, which makes them especially useful for cutting moldings and measuring plywood. In addition, most tape measures come with helpful woodworking information printed on the back of the device. Some even feature locking systems to ensure accurate angles.

While a steel tape measure is the most common tool used in woodworking, it isn't ideal for every project. While it's convenient, it doesn't provide the most accurate measurements, which is why measuring in inches isn't recommended. In woodworking, consistency is more important than accuracy.

Another tool for measuring in woodworking is a short ruler. A six-inch ruler is more convenient to use than a standard tape measure and is more convenient to keep in your pocket. A short rule is also useful for measuring angles on your workpiece.

Another useful tool for measuring in woodworking is a level. Although a level can help you make measurements, it can also point out imperfections. If you don't use a level, you may end up with a frustrating result. Fortunately, using a level can help you achieve perfect work.

The end of the tape should be parallel to the edge, and the tip should be horizontal at the point where you're measuring. This way, the tape won't bend when you drop it.

Marking

Marking is a very important skill for woodworkers. Accurate marking allows woodworkers to build projects faster and with more efficiency. If they fail to mark their work accurately, they may end up building pieces with uneven edges or uneven thickness. Whether you are a beginner or a seasoned woodworker, you can use a variety of marking tools and gauges to achieve your desired results.

A marking gauge is a tool that allows you to make a perfectly shaped line before cutting wood. There are many types of marking gauges available, with different cutting tips and a variety of applications. Steelknife gauges are typically used for scribing across the grain, while knife scribe gauges are used to make clean lines with the grain.

When using a tape measure, it is important to keep the tape parallel to the part you want to cut. Be sure to start your measuring tape from a flat surface.

Then, line up the tape with a line on a ruler or rule. If possible, start at the 10" mark on the tape or rule.

Another essential tool for woodworkers is a try square. A try square is a square that does not cover the full length of a blade. It is used against a work piece to check its squareness and to ensure that it is square and flat. Basic marking tools in woodworking are an essential part of any woodworking project. These tools can be used for delineating parallel lines, marking the center of a piece, and more. Accurate marking tools can help you create professional results. Regardless of whether you're a beginner or an experienced woodworker, having the right marking tools is vital to the success of your project.

Cutting

Cutting is an integral part of woodworking. While sharp tools produce better cuts, blunt ones create less defined cuts. Using a blunt tool causes more surface area to be in contact with the wood, and requires more force to cut. Moreover, blunt tools also result in wider and poorly defined lines. The angle at which a tool cuts the wood also affects the quality of the cut.

A circular saw is another tool that can be used for cutting in woodworking. A circular saw is designed to cut wood, although it can be used for other materials. However, for precise cuts on hardwood plywood, a square-cut teeth or carbide-tipped blade should be used. If you plan to use the saw for other materials, such as metal, it is better to use a jigsaw.

Ripping lumber is another method used to cut wood. Ripping lumber is an activity often performed on a table saw, although it can also be performed with a circular saw. Ripping lumber is difficult to perform properly and errors can have long-term consequences for your project. In general, you should avoid ripping lumber if possible.

The best way to protect your woodwork tools is to keep them clean. Woodworking tools can get dirty if you work in a messy workshop. If your workshop is dirty, it can affect the finished product. If you have a rag on your work area, drape it over a noncombustible item to prevent it from being burned.

Chisels are an important tool for woodworking. A chisel has a sharp edge that makes it possible to cut precise shapes. Some chisels are large enough to cut heavier materials. Chisels are also used for joining pieces together. The best part about chisels is that they can be used for any type of woodworking project.

Before using a table saw, it's important to learn the proper way to use it. A good way to practice with this tool is to choose a simple woodworking project that is not too complicated.

Drilling

There are some methods that will ensure that your holes will look great without causing too much damage. For instance, you can use a depth stop to know how deep to drill. You can also mark the spot where you want to stop drilling with sticky tape.

A benchtop drill press can handle most of your drilling needs and will be much less expensive than a floor-standing drill press. For larger projects, you'll need more sophisticated tools, like drill presses and lathes.

When drilling in wood, it's important to start with a small hole. This will prevent the wood from ripping. Once you've started a small hole, make sure that the drill is in reverse before you try to drill deeper. The reverse drill will cut the wood in the opposite direction. This method prevents the wood from splitting along the grain.

Use pliers to hold the flat end of the spool while you drill. Then, take the drill bit and align it with the start hole. Drilling at an angle will present its own unique set of challenges. When drilling in an angled position, the drill bit will begin to bore, skittering back and forth across the wood. Using a drill guide will make drilling angled holes much easier.

Drilling in wood is a fundamental woodworking technique, but it can be difficult if you don't use the right drill bits. Using the right drill bits will make drilling in wood much easier, and it will prevent your wood from splintering. This will ensure that you drill at the correct speed and prevent splintering.

A flat bit is used to drill a straight hole. A countersink drill bit will create a recess for a screw and prevent the screw head from showing. You can also use a pilot hole, which will allow you to drive a wood screw with less difficulty. Pilot holes are required for larger projects, but they are not essential if you're only drilling twox4s. For faster drilling, you can use self-tapping screws. Alternatively, you can use power screws for rough construction.

Shaping

Shaping in woodworking involves the use of hand tools and power tools. Using power tools is the best choice for rounded corners and beveled edges, but hand tools are also useful for shaping wood parts. The use of rasps and chisels provides a more subtle finish. If you prefer to use hand tools, you can also choose to use hand planes or dovetail saws.

The process of shaping begins by bringing the tool into alignment with the workpiece and repeatedly moving the tool across it in a straight line. The workpiece is gradually fed into the line of motion of the tool, producing a flat, smooth surface. Using a tool for shaping requires practice and a light fingertip grip. Different tools have different eccentricities and react differently to different wood species and grain patterns.

Shaping in woodworking is essential for creating furniture and other pieces. If you want to create beautiful and unique pieces, then you should be familiar with different types of tools and their applications. Shaping in woodworking can also help you create decorative surfaces and joints.

In woodworking, shaping involves using a soft wood to carve out non-rectangular shapes. Soft wood is commonly available and is inexpensive. Pine is an excellent choice because it is cheap and suitable for hand shaping. To test the softness of a wood, try pressing your fingernail into it.

Pattern shaping is a popular woodworking process. It produces precise copies of parts. Using a straight bit with a bearing that matches the cutter's diameter, this process involves running the rough-cut part along the bearing.

Then, you trim off the excess wood and shape the part into an exact copy of the pattern.

Power tools are also popular tools for shaping wood. A tablesaw can cut large-radius cove molding, while a router can cut any shape imaginable. Power tools also have jigs and clamps to hold your workpiece in an unlikely position. Jigs also guide the blade along a delicate edge.

Hand shaping can be relaxing, but can quickly turn into a tedious process if you don't use clamps. In addition, clamping directly to soft wood will leave indentions. To avoid this, place a piece of wood between the clamp and the work. The sacrificial piece will distribute the clamp's weight across the wood and reduce indentions.

Clamping

Clamping in woodworking involves the use of special clamps to secure various pieces together. You can use a variety of different types depending on the purpose. For instance, a corner clamp will hold the pieces together at a 90-degree angle. This type of clamp is useful when building drawers or picture frames. Another type of clamp is a face clamp. This type of clamp comes with a pad to protect the surface of the piece being clamped. It's also useful for holding delicate pieces together for drilling or gluing. Finally, you can use a bar clamp. This style is commonly used to hold two pieces together.

Your workpiece must be properly glued before applying pressure, and the clamp should provide enough pressure without being too tight.

These clamps have big metal protectors, which distribute equal pressure over the entire workpiece. You should make sure to purchase clamps made of maple or oak. They have similar features.

Corner clamps are essential for connecting the corners of a workpiece. A corner clamp pack contains four clamps and a non-slip handle. Its aluminum design offers a better grip and prevents the clamp from slipping out of place.

Another type of corner clamp is a trigger clamp. This type of clamp is easy to use and doesn't require any tools to operate.

Glueing

When glueing in woodworking, you can use a rope clamp to hold the joints together while the glue dries. PVC pipes are ideal for this purpose, because they can be cut into quarter-inch pieces and shaped like a C-clamp.

There are several types of woodworking glue. The most common is the yellow type, also known as aliphatic resin or PVA. This is a cheap, easy-to-find product that dries quickly. It is also a tried and tested product. You can find dozens of varieties of woodworking glue on the market, so it's easy to find one that works for you.

There are several types of wood glues, and each has its own set of pros and cons. Some types are more expensive than others. Titebond III, for example, is more expensive in the long run, but it has a reputation for adhesion. Glueing with PVA will work well for most projects, but it is not a good choice for fine wood projects. If you don't know much about wood glue and how to use it, PVA may be a good option. However, it does require some practice.

Wood glues can be applied using brushes. Flux brushes can be purchased at home centers and hardware stores. They are a convenient way to apply glue to small parts and joints. These brushes are durable and easy to clean. Glues should be used with care, because too much or too little glue can weaken the connection between two pieces of wood. Applying too much glue will waste glue and slow down the curing process. As you gain experience, you will be able to gauge the amount of glue required for different joints.

Too little glue can result in weak joints, while too much glue can create a mess and waste glue. Excess glue should be scraped away after the glue dries. Otherwise, your workpiece may become stuck to the table. Therefore, practice is a key factor.

Water-based glues have an extended working time of 30 to 45 minutes, but you must avoid removing them too soon as it can cause sunken joints.

Fixing

Occasionally, you may have to repair a chip in woodwork. The most obvious woodworking repair involves replacing a damaged piece of wood. While you can use a new piece of wood, the first step is to remove any loose pieces. You can also sand the edge. A shop vac can help remove loose dust, as can a wet tack cloth. Once the area has dried, you can start the repair.

As a woodworker, you will likely make mistakes. Sometimes you might make an error while mortising a piece. Some of these techniques will turn your mistakes into design opportunities. Some even make mistakes invisible. A professional woodworker can offer many solutions to these problems.

In building construction, fixing is an essential part of the process. When you repair a building, you must do two major types of work. First, you must construct the shell of the building. This includes constructing the walls, floors, and ceilings. You must also install plumbing and electrical fittings. Second, you need to finish the building.

The Basics of Sanding and Finishing

The process of sanding and finishing wood is crucial for a variety of reasons. For example, it helps to refine the wood grain and make the surface more receptive to stain or finish. For example, to apply an oil finish, a surface that is sanded down to 220 grit must be prepared. Then, the oil should be applied along the grain of the wood. Once the stain or finish has dried, it's important to remove any excess oil slurry with 320-grit sandpaper.

During the final sanding stage, you'll use your hands to remove orbital scratches from the surface, creating finer scratches that run parallel to the wood grain. While you're sanding, be sure to back up the sandpaper with a sanding block, which keeps the surface flat. The most convenient sanding blocks are rubber blocks, but you can also use cork blocks.

Applying the final coat of stain or finish is another important step in woodworking. It will give your piece that beautiful, shiny finish. If you want to change the color of your piece, you can apply more than one coat of stain or finish. It's important to apply the stain or finish evenly, because excess stain can stain the finish.

For finishing, you'll need a few basic tools. A rag will help you wipe off excess finish and a cloth to wipe the wood clean after sanding. To apply a varnish, you might also need a spray gun.

The right stain or finish will bring your wood project to life and protect it from damage. A good wood finish will protect your work for years. Then, use finer grits and repeat the process. Finally, let your finished piece dry.

While woodworking, you must be careful to clean the area with a microfiber cloth after finishing. You should also use a vacuum cleaner to remove any embedded dust. Afterwards, you can use mineral spirits to clean the wood. Make sure to let it dry thoroughly. If you want a softer finish, use paste wax and a fine steel wool to remove any remaining traces of the previous finish.

Finishing your wood project is essential if you want it to last for many years. Not only will it make your wooden piece more durable, but it will also improve its aesthetic appeal. With care, finishing your wood project will be a joyous and rewarding experience.

The first step in sanding and finishing is removing the old finish. A power sander is the easiest method. For larger surfaces, you may want to use a random orbit sander. You can also use sandpaper or a chemical stripper.

Four Processes Involved in Wood Processing

Wood processing involves several processes. The first one is called "seasoning," which involves reducing the water content in logs. The seasoned wood is then used to make furniture, including kitchen cabinets, in-built cupboards, and decorative wood furnishings. Other uses for seasoned wood include door frames, ceiling wood, and sculptures.

Plain sawing

One of the four main processes involved in the wood processing industry is the plain sawing of wood. This process involves sawing planks on a horizontal plane parallel to the axis of the wood. For example, planks of lumber produced with this method are more susceptible to splitting and warping than other types of lumber.

The basic principle behind the process of plain sawing is to create uniform boards of wood. A log is first split into quarters, and then the sawyer slices the widest board first. Then, the sawyer flips the quarter and cuts the next-widest board. Then, he repeats this process until he reaches the desired yield of boards. This process is very efficient and does not waste a lot of wood. The final product will be quarter-sawn, which is often known as "quartersawn" lumber.

Another major process involved in wood processing is tangential sawing. This technique involves passing the log through a circular blade without changing the angle of the blade. This results in a more stable plank with better stripe figures than one that is made using flat sawing. Another downside of plain sawn timbers is that they are susceptible to cupping, twisting, and bowing. They also absorb moisture and become distorted over time.

This process produces the most common kind of lumber. The annual growth rings of plain sawn lumber intersect at an angle of about 60 degrees to 90 degrees to the surface. This type of sawing is also cheaper than live sawn milling, and produces fewer wastes. However, plain sawn lumber has several structural disadvantages, including the fact that the grain is not vertical on the face of the board.

Seasoning is another process involved in wood processing. A seasoning process is necessary for the wood to be suited for various purposes. Seasoning is a process that helps to retain moisture.

Kiln drying

This process is important because wood can develop defects if the drying process is not done correctly. The defects include end splits, checks, honeycombing, and collapse. Achieving the correct moisture content is critical to the quality of finished products, and kiln drying is a vital part of any wood processing operation.

The kiln's heating system supplies heat, while baffles control air flow. The flow of air is important to remove moisture from the lumber and ensure uniform drying throughout the width of the kiln. The layout of the vent system is unique to each manufacturer. The air intake at one end of the kiln is cool, dry air, while the air exits the other end is warm and moist. Some hardwoods require the introduction of humidity by a steam spray or cold water misting system.

Kiln drying is an essential process in wood processing. It reduces green lumber's moisture content to a "workable" level. Excess moisture in wood can lead to a variety of problems, including warping and splitting. Kiln drying is the first step in moisture control and is the standard practice in wood production mills.

Kiln drying is an effective way to prevent insect infestations and reduce warping and distortion during service. The drying process also hardens resinous softwoods, which are less likely to weep onto the finished product. It also enables paints and other finishes to adhere better. Modern adhesive formulations work best on dry wood, and wood preservatives and fire retardants penetrate the wood better.

Recirculating shred

Recirculating shred is a method of processing wood waste into fine wood chips. It is used to recycle wood waste and to remove metal parts. Typically, it works by sorting the wood into two types: A1 and A2. This method also helps to separate ferrous metal from wood. This is done with a drum magnet installed within the sucking system or an overband magnet installed before re-shredding.

Shred-Tech manufactures shredding equipment that meets regulatory safety requirements.

Parallel strand lumber

Parallel strand lumber is a composite timber product. It is produced from scrap wood and is thicker than traditional lumber. Each strand of wood is 0.8 mm thick and 20 to 50 mm wide. It is then glued and pressed together at high pressure, forming a layered structure that can be bent and shaped. Parallel strand lumber is used as a basic construction material in furniture, flooring, and general construction.

While solid lumber was traditionally the main material for wood buildings, parallel strand lumber has become a popular alternative to solid lumber. The first strand-based products were developed as an alternative to plywood. However, the production of veneer-based EWPs has become increasingly expensive as logs of sufficient quality and size become scarce.

The manufacturing process used to create PSL is similar to that used for conventional lumber, except it uses veneer strands instead of planks. These products are used as girders, posts, beams, headers, studs, and columns. Their attractive appearance makes them an attractive structural material.

Another popular method is using structural composite lumber. These products are made from a composite of strands of wood and are bonded together with moisture-resistant adhesives. These strands are stronger than conventional lumber and provide greater dimensional stability. In addition, SCL lumber is resistant to moisture changes and is ideal for heavy-duty projects.

PSLs require higher bonding pressure and are often heavier than comparable lumber of the same size. Furthermore, they are heavier than their structural counterparts, such as LVLs or glued-laminated lumber. They also have high specific gravity (SG) values.

Parallel strand lumber is one of the four primary types of plywood. These lumber products are used for construction purposes and are made of thin veneers. They are typically three to four mm thick. PSL can be stained and is suitable for exterior use. If the lumber is already dried, it will pass through a planer. This process uses a rotating cutting head to smooth out all surfaces and round off edges. The lumber then undergoes mechanical and visual inspection.

Advantages and Disadvantages

The tangential sawing method is a common method used to cut lumber. Its benefits are obvious: it cuts the lumber into thin strips, thereby reducing costs and maximizing yields. It can also yield higher quality lumber than other sawing methods. However, it does have drawbacks.

Tangential sawing method

The tangential sawing method is used to cut logs at an angle to the growth rings, avoiding splits and cupping. It produces more stable planks and a better stripe figure. However, it has its limitations, making it best suited only for annual rings with good definition.

Cost of tangential sawing method

The tangential sawing method is often used in large scale lumber mills because of its high production rates and reduced cost. It is a highly efficient method for cutting lumber to the exact size that is required for a construction project. However, it does have some disadvantages. For one, the lumber can be very unstable due to tangential grain and can have dimensional instability. To solve this problem, top-quality producers mill and dry the lumber very carefully.

The cost of tangential sawing depends on how much lumber you need. This method is not always the most efficient, but it can give you a high-quality product that is much cheaper than other methods. It requires fewer workers and produces the widest planks with minimal waste.

Quality of tangential sawn lumber

Tangential sawn lumber is more stable and durable than flat sawn lumber. Its grain is tangential, or at a 30 degree angle from the board face, rather than perpendicular. However, it does have some drawbacks, including waste and dimensional instability.

In the process of cutting timber, tangential and radial sawn methods are used to produce different types of wood. This grain pattern is also known as cathedral grain.

While plain-sawn lumber is the most common cut, tangential sawn lumber is often more stable. This type of lumber has a higher yield of lumber, but is also more prone to twist and cupping. Top producers will always mill and store their lumber in a way that minimizes the risk of cupping or twisting.

The tangential sawn lumber quality can be determined by several factors. The first is the ring grain. A board made of tangential lumber will be thinner than one made from straight-grain lumber. This type of lumber also tends to be less expensive. However, it takes longer to produce. Moreover, it involves more waste.

Rift-sawn lumber, on the other hand, is narrower and more stable. Its grain pattern will be more uniform, with no visible flecks in oak. Rift-sawn lumber produces the most waste.

A log's volumetric and tangential shrinkage ratio (T/R) is an important indicator of the wood's stability. Low T/R ratio indicates stable wood species. A high T/R ratio indicates low yields.

The tangential sawn lumber is often more durable than quarter-sawn lumber, which is often characterized by a spotted figure or ribbon stripe. It also has less shrinkage and checking than quarter-sawn lumber. This method minimizes waste and maximizes usable material.

Types of Sawing

There are several different saw types. You might know about the compound saw and the miter saw. Find out which one you should choose for the job at hand.

Compound saw

Compound sawing is a popular way to cut large pieces of lumber. A compound saw allows you to make bevel or miter cuts and can handle a wide variety of materials. It is also possible to use compound saws for cutting metal. The dual compound sliding miter saws feature sliding rails, a beveling wheel, and a miter table. These tools make it easier to make compound cuts and save time.

They are used in joinery or when an angle is desired. When using a compound miter saw, it is important to set the mitre and bevel angles correctly to avoid making a mistake.

A sliding compound miter saw works by pulling the motorhead toward you as you lower the board. This action activates the motor and pushes the saw through the material. They are available in single or dual bevel varieties. Some compound miter saws also come with zero-clearance arms so they can sit close to the wall without limiting their blade travel.

Compound sawing is an excellent choice if you want to create projects that don't look like the work of a scroll saw. You can even use this technique for chess pieces. When using a compound saw, you should ensure that you have a square blank, mark a dotted fold line on the blank, and place a sharp crease on the fold line. When using a compound saw, it is important to keep all of the parts of the saw in their proper positions, so you don't accidentally cut a piece.

It will also include detailed patterns for three-dimensional wood projects. Whether you are looking to make a clock, a candle stick, or anything else, this book will show you how to use a compound saw effectively.

This tool has a 10-inch blade, a laser guide, and 15-amp power. It also has a dust-sucking feature. However, it is rather complicated to set up, and weighs almost 60 pounds. If you are serious about learning compound sawing, you should invest in a quality compound saw.

Compound saws are also safer than miter saws. When using a compound miter saw, you should keep a safe distance from the blade to prevent kick-back. They can also cause injuries to your eyes and hands.

For a multicolored project, you should use a multi-colored construction paper. This material is not expensive in materials but does not come with a good finish. A multicolored piece made of MDF is a great choice if you want to paint it or use a print-on pattern.

The TPI of a saw blade depends on your woodworking plan. A blade with a lower TPI will be able to cut lumber faster. In most cases, a TPI of 60 to 90 will work best.

For more advanced cutting projects, you can use a sliding compound miter saw. This saw is smaller and more portable than a traditional miter saw, but has greater capacity. It also has a sliding mechanism that reduces the amount of heat produced by the blade. These saws can also be used for framing projects.

Chapter 4:
Types of Joints in Woodwork Projects

There are several types of joints you can use in your woodwork projects. These include Dovetail, Box, Pocket-hole, and Tongue and groove. Each has its own pros and cons.

Dovetail

This type of joint is used to make drawers that are both strong and durable.

Dovetail joints are available in many different styles. There are through dovetails, half-blind dovetails, sliding dovetails, and stopped dovetails. Regardless of the type of dovetail you're looking for, they will make your woodworking projects stronger and look more attractive.

Unlike some other types of joints, dovetail joints require no fasteners. This makes them very strong and are also a great choice for furniture construction. However, some woodworkers use adhesive to give them extra support. The large surface area of a dovetail joint means it can be filled with glue without being noticeable.

Box

It is easy to make and can add elegance to your projects. The basic box joint can be made with three simple tools. If possible, mark the top and bottom edges of each piece. After that, cut the waste side of the lines. Once the pieces are cut, smooth the joints using glasspaper. After applying wood adhesive, wipe away any excess glue before it dries. If the timber is thick, use nails to secure it.

Pocket-hole

The first step in making pocket-hole joints is to plan out how you will install them. It's important to make sure the holes are oriented in the right direction to provide the screws with a better bite and hold them securely in place. The spacing between screw holes is also an important consideration, as it will reduce the tendency of the joint to twist out of alignment.

To drive pocket-hole screws, you must use a drill/driver that has a bit-guide.

Tongue and groove

There are a number of ways to use tongue and groove joints in your woodwork projects. First, you'll need a table saw or router. Both of these tools will make it easier to create the joints. You should buy router bits that include both a tongue and a groove cutter.

Tongue and groove joints are very popular in cabinetry because they're sturdy and easy to install. However, they do have their own disadvantages. Because they require minimal assembly, they may not be as durable as other joints. For example, they may not be suitable for thin panels, as they tend to expand and contract during the adhesive process.

Dowel

A dowel joint is a woodwork joint made of dowels. To create a dowel joint, you'll first need two pieces of wood. The two pieces must be sized similarly and have similar thicknesses. In addition, the joints must fit snugly, and the dowels should reach into the other board at the same point. After a fitting is complete, the joint is ready for glue.

When used properly, dowel joints add strength to the materials connected. This allows the joints to withstand pulling and twisting forces. Unlike dovetail joints, dowel joints are easy to add and require less effort. However, it is important to note that dowel joints must be used with care, and they can only be done by experienced woodworkers.

How to Fasten Joning Pieces in Woodwork

If you're working on a project that requires fastening wooden Joning pieces, you should learn how to use the correct kind of screw and nail. In addition, fastening pieces made of too-dry or too-wet wood can lead to cracks and gaps in your project. If you're using nails or screws with the wrong length, you can also damage the joints.

Dowel joints

Woodworkers use dowel joints as an alternative to other methods of wood joinery. They offer the advantage of being fastener-free and secure. In addition, dowels help keep joint parts aligned during the glue-up process. This prevents misalignment and ensures that the pieces are joined correctly.

When creating dowel joints, you should use the correct length. The proper length is about one-half to one-half inch. If your dowel is too long, use a grooved dowel pin to help release excess glue. Also, use a doweling jig to ensure that the holes are exactly square and are the same distance from the work faces.

The most convenient method to make precise dowel joints is to use a doweling jig. This tool comes with a set of holes and removable sleeves for each dowel. Dowel joints are fast, easy, and flexible. The Triton TDJ600 drill bit has a 600-watt motor and a 16-inch drill bit.

Dowel pin

There are a variety of different types of dowel pin, and many different fixing arrangements are available. Some types of wooden furniture may require several types of dowel pins in order to achieve the desired result.

Another common type of dowel pin is a threaded pin. These have a larger surface area than nonthreaded pins and can be more easily glued into place. However, these will tarnish over time. This can be beneficial when joining dark-colored pieces.

When using dowel pins, it is crucial to use the right size. The pin should be approximately 1/3 to half of the thickness of the board.

Dowel rod

They are more durable than screws, but may take a lot longer to install. They are best for joints that aren't very complex, such as right angles and flat angles. However, some applications require more complex joints. Dowels are also useful in metal work and concrete construction.

Wooden dowels are a common tool for woodworking. They also serve as guides when joining pieces of wood. In addition to providing structural reinforcement, dowel joints also look neater because they don't require any other equipment to hold the pieces together.

When using dowels, be sure to use the correct size. A dowel that is too long may force the joint open. To avoid this problem, choose a dowel that is shorter than a board's width. When using longer dowels, make sure they're grooved to help the glue escape. Also, when using dowels, remember to mark the center lines on the adjacent boards before joining them.

A dowel should have a diameter of at least 3/16 inches, and should be at least one inch long. Dowels can be purchased at home centers or made at home.

Conclusion

Instead, have fun and try new methods or tools whenever you can. Or sharpen a particular set of skills and become a master! Either way, take the first step and dive into woodworking! You won't regret learning this noble skill.

Woodworking is a vast, booming market! You can do anything from furniture to model cars, from jewelry to musical instruments.

You can even decorate your house with unique pieces of furniture. And this is just what you get! The possibilities are endless!

BOOK 2: TOOLS

Introduction

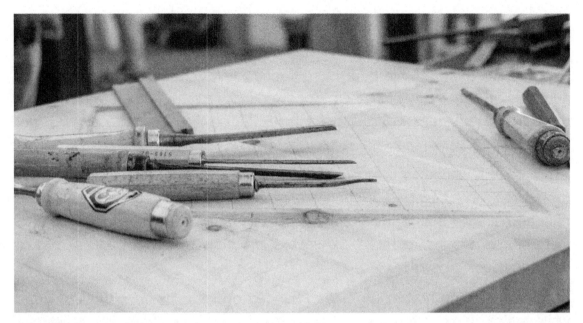

Woodworking is not harmful. It could be less risky than driving. Know how to utilize your tools appropriately by understanding how they operate. Apply common sense.

I think one of the reasons woodworking has grown to be such a tremendously popular pastime in recent years is that it gives people a means to escape the cacophony that currently permeates our lives. When you enter a woodworking shop to construct something, you're only starting off. You may get a sense of how something will feel once you're done by going into the shop with an idea of what you want to accomplish. You can create anything from nothing by employing logic, intelligence, your capacity for problem-solving, and common sense. You take complete responsibility for all aspects of a project, including planning a strategy or building your tools, manufacturing wood and other materials, committing to a course of action, and managing the issues you'll face. It's a successful business.

Woodworking is fun, and you get nice stuff for your house, but it's really about discovering who we are and realizing that, when we take the time to build it, life can provide so many more intrinsic rewards. Set aside a few hours each week to use some power tools.

Architecture, religion, agriculture, leisure pursuits, and survival have all long benefited from woodworking.

People have been able to hunt more successfully, set up tents, make boats, and support life by honing their woodworking abilities. Wood was used to create sculpture as well as household items like furniture, bowls, and spoons. Woodworking aided in societal progress.

Even though wood is important to human survival today, it may be overlooked and devalued in our technologically advanced period. It is a natural resource that is important to our daily activities because so many of them revolve around it. There are several products made of wood all around you if you look closely.

Imagine observing how much it has changed over the last few hundred years while sitting in your toolbox with your daily nail. Tools have improved over time to speed up, increase durability, and improve precision in woodworking jobs.

For many years, people have built houses, cabinets, ships, and furniture using hammers, mallets, saws, planers, calibers, squares, and nails.

I'll walk you through an overview of what woodworking is specifically, along with the equipment, safety precautions, mistakes to avoid, and other things you may anticipate from it, in this tutorial. There are several books that cover this pastime in depth at an expert level, but in this book, we'll look at every aspect of woodworking, from the very beginning to mastery. I'll start by answering the most frequent queries that you could have had as a beginner and are undoubtedly compelled to ask given your foundational knowledge.

The best chance for success would be to start with something simple. When you are familiar with modern equipment and how to work with materials that are now on the market, comparable to those from a few years ago, it is much simpler to start into woodworking and produce some high-quality work. The best option is to employ the woodworking technique if you want high-quality, extremely durable genuine wood furniture but don't want to pay for a kit to acquire it.

I assure you that woodworking is a wonderful hobby, so why don't you just unwind while using this book? In time, you could emerge as the subsequent woodworking guru.

Chapter 1:
Woodworking Tools

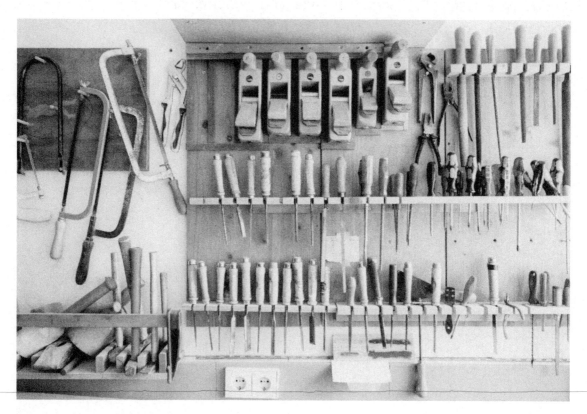

The Claw Hammer

Let's begin with the most fundamental tool found in every home that is the claw hammer. The claw on the opposite end of the head must be balanced by the final head, which must be slightly more rounded.

Another type of head is called a waffle head. It is most often used in construction the waffle head leaves a distinct waffle pattern on the wood after it is driven. It is, however is not the ideal nail for woodworking.

The most popular clawhammer is 20 pounds. size. It's strong sufficient to push nails yet is easily maneuverable by pulling nails with ease.

While wooden handles look lovely but they might not be able to withstand the stress if you need to drag a lot of nails.

However, they will not take the vibrations of driving nails in the same way that the handle made of hickory can. It is also important to actually make sure the metal or fiberglass handles are equipped with a rubber grip for convenience and control. If you're driving lots of nails, the wood hand-held hammer will work ideal for reducing strain on your wrist and hand also.

The Tape Measure

Choose a retractable one that has at least 25 feet in length. There is a problem getting it to fold back more than that.

As measurements on large-scale projects can be vulnerable to even tiny measurement deviations It is important to make sure that the "hook" or tab on the end is secure and has no room for. There could be up to 1/8" deviation when they become loose with your measurements. This could cause serious accuracy issues over the long haul.

The Utility Knife

A high-quality utility knife is a great tool for woodworkers. There are a variety of different types but the type which uses disposable blades is most commonly used. Blades retract into grip for security. The woodworker can use the utility knife to clean out mortise joints, or cutting wood, as for a variety of other purposes.

The Moisture Meter

A top-quality wood moisture gauge is crucial to the long-term viability of any woodworking project that you make. Lumber mills attempt to dry their runs of lumber based on the final destination of the product. For instance, if lumber is harvested from the moist Northeast and then shipped to the dry

Southwest the wood will dry more quickly than lumber that was stored in the Northeast to be used by woodworkers.

The achievement of your woodworking project from flooring made of wood to kitchen cabinets, to furniture of the highest quality, is contingent on the right moisture content of the woods you choose to cover your region of the nation.

Some moisture meters feature pins that go through the wood's surface. They can cause tiny holes which scratch the surface and need to be filled. Other models are not pin-less. They are equipped with sensing plates which scan the wood underneath.

Look for one that makes use of technology that isn't affected by the moisture levels of the wood's surface within the timber, for instance, Wagner's moisture meters that use IntelliSense(tm) technology.

The Chisel

A variety of Chisels should be a part of every workstation. Chisels aren't just for woodcarvers. Anyone who works with wood will actually require Chisels to remove dust from joint joints and saw cuts. Choose chisels made from carbon steel with high-alloy or chromium vanadium alloyed steel.

Handles made of hardwood are the best particularly if they feature metal caps. This can prevent the end on the grip from bending as you hammer it.

There are a number of sizes, in 1/4 " increments that range from 1/4 " up to 1.25 ". The smallest chisels work best for mortise-work. They are 1/4 " or 1" are ideal for door hinges, while one 1/2 " works great for chipping out. It is possible to purchase the corner chisel to cut into the wood by hitting it with the force of a hammer. It's as a hole punch.

Most chisels are beveled along both sides as well as the cutting edge. However, special chisels are cut with a bevel at an edge that cuts. The bevel is 20-25 degrees down all the way down on the one side and flat on the actual back side. The blade will measure somewhere between four" between 7 and 4" in length.

The Level

Each woodworker requires at least two levelers. Typically, you'll require the 8" level as well, which is commonly called a torpedo-level.

The Screwdriver

Screwdrivers are another item that should be included for the woodworker's collection of hand tools. A high-quality construction is essential to an effective assortment of screws. Then, the moment you first apply the slightest "oomph" into them, they splinter away and become unusable.

It is recommended to use an extended screwdriver that has an angled blade that's extremely durable. This provides a lot of torque. Also, you'll need an intermediate and small slot screwdriver.

When working with cabinets or other tight areas when woodworking, you'll require the right screwdriver that has a narrow shank to access screws that are located in deep holes.

Take a few medium Phillips screwdrivers with heads and an stubby one for those places that are tight.

The Nail Set

The hand tool that each woodworker needs is the nail set. They resemble awls and are used to insert nail heads into wood to ensure they're flush or to the edge. This lets you make holes, and then make them ready for painting or staining.

The nail setter will typically feature a convex, or concave surface that can hold the nail more securely and prevent it from slipping off and causing damage to the wood.

The Sliding Bevel

If you're measuring multiple angles using an adjustable sliding bevel or T-Bevel will be an excellent tool. It can be adjusted, and you can even lock it at the angle you wish to mark.

The Layout Square

The design squareor mix square is available in sizes of 6" as well as twelve" sizes. A majority of woodworkers choose the 6" model because it's easier to transport around. Additionally, the majority of wood you'll work with is only 6" wide, which means 12" isn't enough.

Layout squares are essentially a triangular shape that you could use for marking square cut marks on your stock. When you've measured your cut's length you align the layout square to an edge on the wood. The shorter side gives you a straight rectangular cut along the top grain.

This can be helpful when measuring the bevel of the table saw or marking the cut for miter saw. You could also make use of your layout square to measure an angle already in place. Plastic ones are not only fragile, but also tend to warp, which makes them useless.

The Hand Plane

Hand planes hand-plane is the key to the versatility of your woodworking. It is possible to flatten a piece of wood, then add an angle to it, or square the work. Chamfer or shape your stock by using an instrument called a block plane.

Make use of a tiny amount of oil onto the stone that sharpens and then place that bevel in place against the stones. The heel should be raised a bit and then polish it. Turn the blade and rub it against the stone's flat side. The burr will fall off. The cap screw is what holds your blade and that's where you can adjust the depth of the plane you'd like to cut.

If you're doing precise work, you'll need to measure the blade around 1/16". For more general tasks it's up to 1/16". If you plan to finish grain by plane and both ends, smooth them towards the middle in order to prevent cutting the edge on the outside.

The Caliper

The use of calipers is essential for fine-tuning your woodworking project. There are even digital calipers today that make it clear which side you were on or outside of the line. However, metallic ones are always preferred over ones made from plastic, even though the plastic ones are more affordable.

Calipers feature the appearance of a double "F" look. On one side is a huge "F" that is that is used to measure the exterior the object. It is possible to loosen the screw in order to shift the upper "lip" that is the part of the caliper.

Inside calipers will be used to determine the diameter of slots holes' diameters, slot diameters, and dado widths among other things. There's also a depth gauge at the middle of the calipers which can be used to actually determine the depth of the slots and holes. Simply place the caliper's end at the edges of the opening, and move the thumbscrew till it reaches the top in the hole. After that, you can get your measurement. If you want to determine the precise thickness of something that has been attached on a surface you can use calipers to measure the measurement of thickness. You can do this by placing the caliper's butt edge against flat surfaces and using the inside caliper lip that is closest to your palm to measure what the surfaces of the object you're measuring. The distance between the back of that lip to the tip of the caliper will be how thick the object that you're measuring.

While calipers measure as small as 1/1000th of an inch in length, it's likely that you don't require that tight tolerance. Keep in mind that since wood is an organic materialand expanding and contracting according to the humidity levels and changes in temperature. The sizing of the piece to 1/1000ths of a millimeter won't give the wood enough room for air circulation.

The Clamp

There are clamps that can be used for joints with 45 or 90 degrees and pipe clamps that extend long distances. The typical way to purchase pipe clamps and put your own pipe in the fixtures to build a sturdy clamp of the size you require. C-clamps and F-clamps are the norm, however now there are K camps as well. One of the advantages of K camps is that they extend a considerable distance into the work space and secure things within the middle of your work area. Bar clamps with deep-throated bellows as well as C clamps can aid in this.

It is impossible to live without the availability from quick grip clamps that come in different sizes. They are made with spreaders that measure 12" or more, and go down to micro-mini clamps suitable for toy construction. A clamp for edges will secure laminate trim to an edge on a table top. A strap clamp can be wrapped around any shape and then pull the joints in. Spring clamps are useful for holding the piece in place. The primary distinction between quick clamps and spring clamps is that quick clamps can be moved into place using just one hand. After release they will lock in the position you want them to be in. Spring clamps are similar to large clothespins.

Hand Screw Clamps are the traditional-looking wooden clamps that have screw awl that is turned from both sides in order to apply equally pressure. They are ideal to apply a lot of pressure to flat or tapered pieces. They do as the name suggests They help you to assemble squares. There are also bench clamps as well as "dogs," as well as other vises and clamps which attach to your work bench.

The Jig Jig

It is not necessary to measure every joint or cut when you've got Jigs. Many woodworkers build themselves jigs. It is usually used that is powered by a tool to direct the piece through the saw. You can create an jig you can make the perfect circle. Perhaps you want to build furniture with legs that taper. A jig is a great tool for this with no hassle marking the angles of each leg. Dovetail jigs do just that , it helps guide the wood you use to make dovetail joints.

The Hand Saw

A top-quality hand saw must not be ignored. In reality, a good selection of hand saws could be among the most beneficial accessories to your woodworking workshop. It is not necessary to put a powersaw on everything. In fact, you'll probably not wish to. You must be able for the feel of the wood's reaction to the saw blade as well as the blade's reaction to wood. In addition to a coping and Tenon saw, you could need a dovetail or hand miter saws also. In reality, for the majority of woodworkers, having a good selection of Japanese saws is the foundation of their work.

To get started begin with a fretsaw that is suitable for woodworkers. It's similar to an coping saw for wood. You'll need a mini saw also for those places where the chisel won't be able to work. A good Tenon saw is required and an miter box is compatible along with the tenon. Others saws with their various of cutting angles and cutting surfaces, are available when the necessity arises.

The Feather Board

Featherboards are crucial to achieve smooth, professional cuts. They are used with any type of saw as well as other surfaces for cutting to move the materials further than cut edges. You can create the feather board yourself or buy them. Many woodworkers prefer to create them in a way that they fit their individual requirements.

The Metal Detector

You're not searching for treasures hidden in you metal detector. You're searching for something which can ruin your treasures, specifically, your tools for woodworking. It's vital to keep metal off your cutting surfaces or else you'll end up damaging bits, blades, and even knives in your tool. A quick scan using metal detectors will tell you the presence of a piece of nail or screw stuck in your tool stock. The chances are you'll discover it but it's important to know this prior to destroying your tools.

Chapter 2:
Categorization of
Woodworking Tools

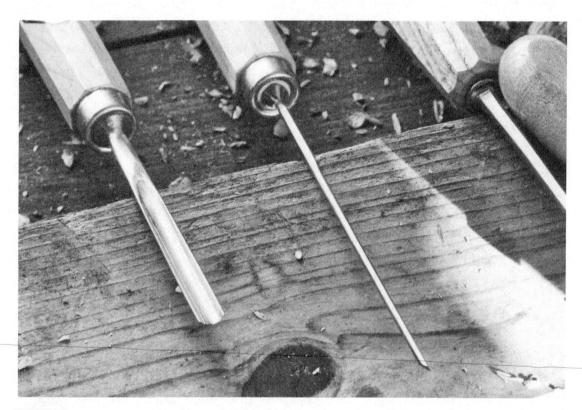

There are a number of tools used in woodworking and they all serve specific purposes. The primary tool in any woodworking project is the plane, although other tools such as a try square and a ruler are essential as well. A woodworker's kit should include four basic planes: the smooth plane, the block plane, the jointer plane, and the jack plane. Typically, these tools have a specific file number and are classified according to their shape and use.

Clamps are an important woodworking tool. A clamp can hold two or more pieces of wood together while a screw or adhesive is applied. A C-clamp is a popular choice as it can clamp two flat pieces of wood together or a workpiece to a worktable.

Functions

Woodworking tools can perform various operations and are very important for a woodworker. Other tools are more versatile, such as router planes, which are useful for a wide variety of finishing jobs.

The oldest tool in the trade, the hand planer, is used for rough work and as a detailer for finishing steps. These tools have a flat stock and metal blades attached to a diagonal handle. The hand plane works by pushing a metal blade across a flat surface to remove wood evenly. A skilled craftsman can also use a hand planer to create rounded edges on wood.

Another tool that is indispensable for woodworking is the table saw. This machine is used for straight cuts in long boards and lumber. This machine is similar to a circular saw, except that it is fixed to the table surface. It also has a metal bar that comes in contact with the lumber.

Modes of action

A woodworking tool's mode of action and function are an important part of the craft. Some tools are specifically used for a specific purpose, while others are used to perform a wide range of tasks. It is also useful for drawing straight lines and measuring small distances on a wooden surface. A metal ruler is usually sturdier than its plastic counterpart, and will stay straighter for longer.

Cost

Woodworking tools can be expensive, but if you do your research, you can buy most of them for less than $100. Basic tools are also necessary, like a handplane and a handsaw. Handplanes are useful for smoothing the wood surface. Other basic tools include a screwdriver set and a hand drill. Clamps are also essential for holding workpieces.

Where to buy

If you're wondering where to buy woodworking tools at a great price, you have a couple of options. One is to look online for auctions that are held by local companies. These auctions are known as Personal Property auctions and can be very helpful in locating woodworking tools for sale. These companies usually list their listings online every week and give consumers two or three weeks to make a bid. These companies also encourage consumers to examine the products before they place a bid on them.

Chapter 3:
Types of Hand Tools

Some of the most common tools include screwdrivers, pliers, and hammers. Other tools can include splitting axes and hatchets.

Hand tools are implements that are used in manual operations, including cutting, sawing, filing, and forging. Common examples include screwdrivers, hammers, and ratchet sets. Utility knives are another example. The types of hand tools available depend on the job. Each hand tool has its own use.

The engineering department aboard a ship is a great example of where hand tools are used. These tools should be handled with caution and taken care of properly. Not only are these hand tools found on board a ship, but they can also be found at machine shops and shipyards.

Multi-purpose tools

A multi-tool is a unit that combines a number of functions into a single device. These can vary in size from small credit card sized multi-tools to larger keyring-mounted and trouser pocket tools. Depending on the size and shape, they are designed for convenience and portability.

These tools can be used for a wide variety of tasks, from slicing ropes to cutting clothes and bandages. They can also be used as a wrench, allowing you to hold the tool handle in one hand and twist your wrist to turn the tool freely.

These multi-tools can be tucked into a pocket or tackle box. They come with a full set of tools for almost any situation, including a knife, tweezers, and scissors. Some tools are designed for the outdoors and may even include a bottle opener or awl. The tools are made of 100 percent stainless steel and have a 25-year manufacturers' warranty.

Pliers

Pliers are a hand tool that can be used to grip a wide variety of items. Some types of pliers feature locking jaws to help prevent accidental opening. Channellock pliers, for example, feature a grooved joint to adjust the opening of the jaws.

Pliers are made of steel alloys, sometimes with other materials added for durability. They are also equipped with metal handles and usually have insulated grips to protect them from electrical shocks. While the basic design of pliers is similar, the pliers come in different sizes and shapes. A plier has a flat, adjustable jaw section with cutting edges and a locking mechanism.

Screwdrivers

Generally, they have an ergonomic design with an oval, square, or hexagonal handle to provide better grip and control. Some types also feature a reversible ratchet action and interchangeable tips.

A screwdriver's shaft is commonly made of strong steel with a short hexagonal section at the top. This adds stability and can increase the torque applied by the tip. Some screwdrivers feature a flat bar section adjacent to the handle, which can be used for additional torque. An offset screwdriver features a handle set at an angle to the blade, giving it additional torque and access to small spaces.

Hatchets

A hatchet is a hand tool that can be used for cutting wood. These tools have a long, curved handle and can be used for a variety of tasks. They are also useful for starting fires without a lighter.

A hatchet is also called a chisel. The blade is longer and wider than other hand tools. It is often beveled on one side. A hatchet is useful in cutting enamel.

Splitting axes

A splitting maul is a type of hand tool used to split logs into kindling. It is similar to a felling axe but has a much longer wooden handle. A splitting maul weighs around eight pounds.

Hammers

They have several different heads, including claw hammers, sledge hammers, and ball peen hammers. Depending on the use for a hammer, it can be used for any application, from hammering nails into wood to shaping metal.

Pliers with needle-nose ends

Pliers are among the most basic hand tools, and they can be used for a variety of tasks. For example, they are great for holding things firmly and can bend wires and remove nails.

These hand tools are great for wire-shaping, making sharp bends and angles, and are available in various lengths. Similar to eyelet pliers, these tools have long or short noses, which makes them useful for affixing grommets or securing them. These pliers are particularly useful for working with wire in electrical boxes. They feature a serrated gripping surface on the nose and a side-cutting edge at the throat.

Adjustable wrench

Its size is usually specified in terms of overall length and jaw capacity. Wide mouth spanners tend to have the largest jaw capacity. Some adjustable wrenches are reversible, with a different type of jaw on one end.

They are generally adjustable, but some models are designed with locking mechanisms to ensure that the wrench maintains its grip on the fastening and reduces hand fatigue. Some wrenches have teeth that are designed to grip smooth round pipes, while others are designed to fit hexagonal fittings or other types of tubes.

Jigsaws

They are flexible and are used to create curved cuts. However, they are not as flexible as circular saws, and are not ideal for cutting straight lines. Before using a jigsaw, be sure to mark the workpiece first. Using a pencil, mark the shape that you wish to cut.

Jigsaws come in many different sizes and types, and their blades can cut a variety of materials. A jigsaw blade with a high TPI will provide a smoother cut and require less sanding. A lower TPI blade will give a faster, coarser cut. There are also multipurpose blades available for use on a variety of materials.

Jigsaws are ideal for cutting wood into shapes, but they can also be used on ceramic tile, sheet metal, and plastic. Jigsaws are also useful for cutting circles of different shapes and sizes. With the right blade and a straightedge, a jigsaw can produce perfect cuts.

Chapter 4:
Assemblage Tools

While putting together wood pieces, accuracy and precision cannot be discarded. Some tools needed to keep these in check are:

The Power Drills

Invest in an advanced drill capable of more control and features; this will get you ahead in your woodworking.

The Screw Guns

Screw guns are important for fastening screws, especially to fast pace a project with multiple screwing.

The Hammers

Hammers occur in different forms and shapes, depending on what they are built for. As a beginner in woodworking and other woodworkers in general, one must first understand the type of hammer needs before purchase.

The Mallets

Mallets are often compared with hammers, but this is, in fact, very erroneous; mallets are used on chisels, they give just the right amount of pressure needed for the chisel to carry out its function while absorbing the rest of the unwanted force. Hammers, on the other hand, are made only for striking. A mallet is also a compulsory item in your toolbox but must never be compared or used in place of a hammer or a hammer in place of a mallet.

Chapter 5:
Sharpening Tools

Typically, whetstones are offered as rectangular blocks-- called bench stones-- for sharpening regular tools or as little knife edges or teardrop section stones for sharpening gouges and etching chisels. Blades could additionally be sharpened on a completely flat metal plate which has actually been cleaned with abrasive powder.

Oilstones

The course, mottled-gray Soft Arkansas stone gets rid of metal rapidly and is utilized for the initial edged tool shaping. Even finer is the uncommon translucent variety. Artificial oilstones are created from sintered silicon carbide or aluminum oxide. Classified as medium, coarse and fine, manufactured sharpening stones are far more affordable than their natural equals.

Waterstones

Since it is reasonably soft and crumbly, a sharpening stone which is lubricated with water cuts quicker than a comparable oilstone; fresh abrasive particles are exposed and discharged continuously as a meta blade is rubbed over the waterstone surface. Nevertheless, this soft bond additionally makes a waterstone susceptible to unintentional damage, particularly when sharpening narrow chisels that might score the surface. Naturally occurring waterstones are so pricey that the majority of tool providers provide just the synthetic varieties that are almost as effective.

Diamond Stones

Very resilient coarse-- and fine-grade sharpening 'stones' consist of a nickel-plated steel plate which is implanted with monocrystalline diamond particles and bound to a rigid polycarbonate foundation. These quick-cutting sharpening tools, offered as narrow files and bench stones, could be utilized lubricated with water or dry. Diamond stones are going to sharpen carbide and steel tools.

Chapter 6:
Tips and Tricks for
Woodworking

I still look for shortcuts to save time or to make my life easier. Over time I have found a different way to do something that I have done a hundred times before, and I wonder why it was never easier for me to discover.

Below are ten woodworking tips that I have acquired from experts, or on my own. These tips are easy but effective ways to keep wood organized and functional.

Wood Layout Triangle

Registration

It's easy to mix wood pieces when you lay them, especially when you have several cuts of a similar length. If the pieces are shifted, you can quickly visualize their position with each other, because only one way is to make the triangle shape together.

Set a triangle on your wood when it sits in the right position to ensure that part of the triangle hits all the pieces that you want to register.

Story Stick

Precise measurements are necessary, but repetitive measurements can easily be minimized by making a story stick, a measuring guide easily usable from any square scrap.

Use a story stick as usual, but open the calculated mark this time. You can now use your story stick as a guide for drilling.

Drill Depth

Not every hole boiled must be entirely through the stuff. While it's easy to set up stops on a drill press, it is quite often the best tool (portability, material size, etc.) to use the press.

Glue Cleanup

Glue is an excellent tool for many woodworking projects. The application of glue is easy, but a little mess can regularly occur. When the adhesive is still warm, cleaning the glue is as easy as spreading the sawdust on the adhesive and rubbing it around to remove the excess adhesive. This is a better way of extracting glue from a damp tissue or sponge because moisture can cause wood swelling.

Cleaning your hands is even easier. When your hands are covered, you can remove it quickly by just rubbing your hands together. The wet or still moist adhesive should flake off.

Wax Paper Cover

It is easier to unroll more wax paper than I feel I would need to cut it to the particular form while it's underworked, rather than to use the clamped edge on the roll. A shop ruler works very well to rub a clean edge on wax paper.

Hold Glue-Ups Instantly

Sometimes a pin doesn't fit into the part I have to glue, and sometimes I'm too eager to wait until the wood adhesive has been placed before I move into the next part of the build. For these situations, hot glue is a big crutch to use for wood.

Stick in your warm glue tool and let it exceed the temperature before applying some wood glue.

When the wood glue has been applied, apply a heat glue squirt to the wood glue gaps. Place the wood parts together and keep in place for a few seconds until the warm glue can be placed.

Sandpaper Organization

I have all sorts of abrasive paper on hand if I need a particular form. As such, my stock of sandpaper is a mess. Since practically all sandpapers are the same size as printer paper, I keep them all in a cheap accordion-type file folder.

I pulled out the package with all my sandpaper and sorted it by grit. Every grate has its folder slot, and the front pouch is reserved for smaller sandpaper scraps.

Chapter 7: Common Woodworking Mistakes and How to Avoid Them

When attempting to assemble the carcass, very tiny variations will cause your drawers to not match.

Then disregard the design's size and function from the carcass. It indicates that the dimensions of your drawer or door correspond to those of the carcass.

A Table that Rocks

The majority of the time, after you finish building a table, it wobbles. (However, it is possible that most woodworkers have experienced the same experience.)

You must verify that the table is square when you stick it up. Assemble the table leg/rail assembly in two steps: first, glue the small rails into the legs, and then, after completely dry, insert these two assemblies into the long rails.

Wood that Splits When Being Cut

To avoid tear-out, place the back edge of the wood as it is cut. The backup wall functions as a sacrificial frame. Make the first and second rips cross-cutting if you have both a rip and a cross-cutting surface. You don't need to consider a back-up wall because the blade is unlikely to shatter on a rip cut.

Joints that are Too Loose

A joint frequently fits too loosely. The loss of flexibility is a particularly challenging issue when dealing with mortise and tenon joints, whose strength is determined by the tightness between mortise and tenon.

Conclusion

Woodworking can be an extremely satisfying and possibly even life-changing interest! But being good at woodworking doesn't come naturally to everyone. As stated earlier, woodworking involves some form of advanced technology and techniques that must be diligently taught and adopted with time and dedication to be made. The time spent studying and practising proper craftsmanship should yield impressive positive results.

The key to a great end product is the right starting material. The main quest of all woodworkers is to learn how to get the most beautiful and workable thing out of the tree and, just as importantly: what isn't possible but is still interesting to look at. We aim to reach the best result we can with a given piece of wood that we have at hand as long as that piece has a usable body and straight grain. We work to a certain standard, which we cannot always meet, but we strive to keep improving.

A wise woodworker once said, "Never get stuck with a piece you like more than you need."

The learning curve involved in making anything is steep, but with time, proper woodworking technique and attention to detail, you can master it.

BOOK 3: PROJECTS

Introduction

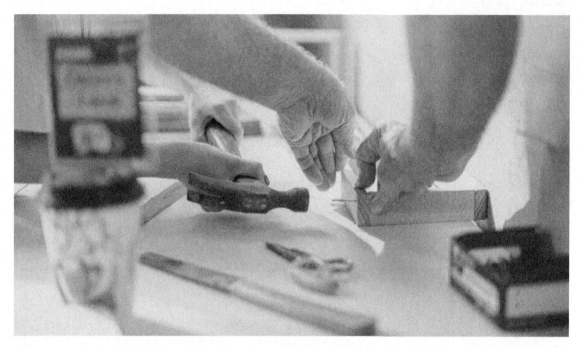

I f you're a beginner in the woodworking world, you should know that there are plenty of woodworking projects you can try. Some of these projects are even suitable for kids, and they don't require a fancy hybrid saw.

Coffee tables are one of the most popular woodworking projects, and there are a variety of styles to choose from. Big square coffee tables are always popular, but you can also try building a rectangular or oval coffee table. The project requires basic woodworking tools and an 8-foot-long 2x4.

Getting started

Getting started with woodworking projects can be fun, but it requires some planning and effort. It also requires you to understand how pieces fit together and which methods to use. The best place to find information and guidance is on the internet. Before you start making furniture or building anything large, consider the purpose of the project and what skills you have.

It is best to take it slow, start with simple projects, and don't try to build complicated structures right away. By working slowly, you'll soon learn the necessary techniques.

Basic tools

There are several basic tools that you must have for woodworking projects. Another basic tool is a thickness planer. While you can buy a benchtop planer, it's best to use a larger one for bigger projects.

Designing your project

When you start woodworking, the first thing you should do is sketch out the general direction of the project. Then, identify the materials needed to complete the project. Most projects are made of a mixture of wood types, and you will need different tools for these projects than you would need for a solid wood project.

If you're a beginner, you can use free software like SketchUp, which lets you create 3-D models of your project. This software is extremely user-friendly and can help you visualize your project and make a rough estimate of the costs involved.

Cost of materials

When planning your woodworking project, the cost of materials can be the determining factor. The cost of materials can range from 10 to 30 percent of the total cost. This cost includes labor, materials, and overhead costs, as well as time spent shopping, choosing boards, loading and unloading equipment, and storing materials. If you are planning to hire a woodworker, make sure to factor in the cost of materials plus their hourly rate.

The cost of materials is an integral part of any woodcraft project. While the price of lumber is relatively constant across the country, the price of a single plank of cedar or oak wood can be more than $100. Likewise, the cost of materials for a coffee table can range from $50 to $150.

Chapter 1:
Basic Wood Work Projects

After a while, pursuing preparations for the next project in woodworking might get a little dull. Often the most successful designs to be designed and marketed come in the form of entirely original concepts. Below are several popular, quickly adjustable, woodworking projects to create and sell.

Three-Legged Stool

The three-legged stool is the epitome of informal furniture, suitable for a quick seat in the kitchen or store, or for a longer sit when the body is leaning forward and partially supported by a desk or counter. For a turner, the stool may be an introduction to joinery as well as an opportunity to branch out from traditional turned work.

Specific box housing

It is commonly regarded as a bedside cabinet, but such products can be scaled up or down to any size and used elsewhere in the home. Because they are so flexible, these projects are among the most successful woodworking projects to be designed and sold.

It is a blueprint of a product, but talk of how you would make something your own to sell at a higher price point. When are you supposed to take someone's name or a strong template and place it on the surface?

Creating and marketing premium items like this will benefit customers who are searching for a great present. They're always searching for fun stuff they can get for free, so this is a common one they might buy.

Floating Shelves

Small homes must make the most of every inch available, even the space behind the walls.

Floating shelves may be purchased in shops or online for $20 to $80 per. However, before you do so, consider making your own. You can obtain the precise size, thickness, and style you desire for around the same price. You may even have them finished to match your decor or furnishings.

Workbench

A workbench is a strong, flat, smooth, molded surface that comes in a range of sizes and shapes to accommodate certain applications. They can be quite sophisticated for engineering design work, complex machining, and elaborate precision tooling, or they can be well finished wood tables for woodworking, metal work, and project design.

Wall planter

Potted plants offer a host of health advantages which explains why so many of our homes have a house. People enjoy charging money (sometimes a lot) to get them in adorable holders strategically positioned around the home. When you are going to sell these, you can make a good win.

One way to use discarded bits of wood to build awesome furniture projects is this wall planter. Because of the strain at the roof, they may carry only smaller plants like succulents. But you can create them with smaller different openings, if you like, and have a whole wall garden!

DIY Nightstand Mid-Century

Add flair to your mid-century classy furnishing room. It might look intricate but most furniture from the middle of the century is a simple DIY away. Take for example the nightstand.

Doormatt wooden

Home is actually where the heart is, so your entrance can look nice as well. Through adopting this video, you will do exactly enough to make your very own wooden doormat, a perfect way to dry off damp shoes without having a soggy pad.

Serving tray for wood cutting machine

Certain contextual concepts to market for successful woodworking ventures are those produced for a dual intent. For starters, you would notice a cutting board can be quickly converted into a fantastic serving tray for cold cutting. Building one isn't really complex, it just takes some time to put together slabs of wood (or use a whole slice).

The only items that can turn a chopping board into an efficient serving tray are handles and a drip shield. To render things ever more presentable, etch and chisel any patterns onto the flat surface.

Wood for furniture

We're not going to limit what furniture you should be making, just go for your creativity. Anything bigger will still receive more cash return and it's just a chance to highlight your different and special talents for other woodworkers with experience creating other items.

Show off your own theme, and may create a whole living room or bedroom package. Customized furniture is one of the most popular wood product concepts to create and market.

Chapter 2:
Choosing What to Construct

The initial step of any woodworking undertaking involves preparation. A straightforward project might take simply a little bit of planning before you're prepared to build, however more complex furniture typically takes a lot more preparation. In either case, certain degree of preparation is important.

Project preparation has 3 standard phases: identifying what to build, figuring out the details via prototypes and illustrations, then determining components and cutting lists from your drawings.

You could create any table you desire and personalize it to fit your individual requirements or tastes. Creating one yourself enables you to manage the quality and expense. Perhaps you simply wish to try some brand-new woodworking methods or tools to broaden your skill base. The inspiration to construct something has a variety of sources.

Gathering ideas-- whatever your inspiration might be for constructing something, odds are you have actually already thought about it sufficiently to have some first ideas about layout. The idea-gathering phase is a crucial one. It's time to let your creativity go without devoting to any idea. Feed your ideas with a great deal of concrete choices so you are able to begin to define a design.

Furniture shops are fantastic locations to analyze various instances of different styles and kinds of furniture. Take a look at family and friends furniture, clip out pictures from magazines and brochures and have them in a idea folder of what you wish to construct.

Furniture follows certain classical design patterns and always has. Definitely, everything you create does not need to comply with an accepted design, however fundamental furniture style is the end outcome of centuries of experimentation. Examine proportions of tables, cabinetry, chests and chairs to get a feeling for how furniture works in conjunction with the body.

Assess your abilities, instruments and budget-- maintain your skill level in mind as you examine the furniture. Furniture with relief carvings, delicate inlays or elements which joins at curves or angles are going to be harder to construct than pieces with direct lines and minimal decoration. These are excellent choices for constructing durable furniture without requiring sophisticated woodworking abilities or a complete toolbox of equipment or instruments.

Attempt a brand-new method occasionally within the furniture design to keep each undertaking exciting. Your roster of abilities is going to grow gradually without endangering the success of an entire project.

Building prudently indicates working with a form of project budget plan in mind. When your pockets for a venture aren't deep, the dollars are going to go further by constructing with 3/4 inch lumber instead of thick pieces of exotic hardwood. It's generally correct that the bigger your project ends up being physically, the more it costs.

Sheet products are typically cheaper and you could stay away from the wood movement problems you'll deal with when developing panels made from strong wood. Before starting a project, take a look around your workshop at the instruments you have. Do you have all the tools you are going to require for cutting out your project components, forming the edges, smoothing the part surfaces or putting togetherpanels? If your project components are curved and little, how are you going to securely cut the small curves?

A scroll saw is the most ideal instrument for this job. Are you going to require one or can you customize the layout or achieve the job another way? Think through the building phase of the venture and how you'll handle each machining action. Otherwise, you might wind up midway through the task and baffled over how to continue. If you can't complete the task without purchasing a brand-new tool, is your budget going to support the expense?

Chapter 3:
Woodworking Projects

Home Furnishing

1. Work Bench

 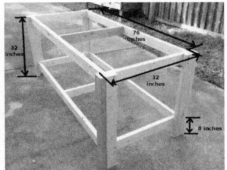

What you need:

- 2x2s for the frame and legs
- 2 x4 lumber for the frame
- 1/4" plywood that would serve as a workbench top
- Circular saw
- Bar clamps
- Chisel
- Square
- Hand drill
- Screws
- Wood glue

How to make it:

✓ Cut the legs. The length has to be 78 centimeters long. Use a measuring tape and a pencil to mark the wood.

✓ Now, you need to cut the pieces that connect the legs. Cut four 2 x 4 pieces that's about 55 centimeters long. Then, assemble the frame by screwing and nailing the pieces together.

✓ Then, drill on each edge of the frame and attach the legs. Then, place the screws in the pre-drilled holes.

✓ Then, screw the rails to the legs. It's easier to do this if the bench is lying on its side.

✓ Cut the plywood to fit the size of the frame. Then, screw the top of the workbench from the below.

2. Three-Legged Stool

What you need:

- Pine log
- Screws
- Power Sander or Sand Paper
- Varnish
- Band saw
- Planer
- Three aspen logs
- Knife
- 3 aspen logs
- Hammer
- Nails

How to make it:

- ✓ Cut a piece of wood from the log using a chainsaw
- ✓ Trim the wood into about two inches thick.
- ✓ Mark a circle on the wood and cut the circle using a band saw
- ✓ Then, flatten the surface using a planer. Then cut three 14-inch aspen logs. This will serve as the legs of your stool.
- ✓ Peel the aspen logs using a knife. Then, sand them.
- ✓ Nail the legs to pine log using a hammer. Then, paint the stool with varnish. Let it dry.

3. Quirky Office Desk

 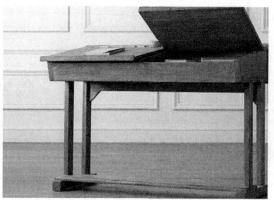

Wht you need:

- Pallets
- Extra poles for the legs
- Paint
- Hammer
- Nails
- Stain
- Saw
- Pencil
- Measuring tape

How to make it:

✓ Remove all of the wood from one pallet and cut the board lengths in half. Screw them into place on the second pallet, then sand it down to prevent splinters.

✓ Check for cracks or rough places before staining. Flip the object over when the stain has dry.

✓ Paint all four poles your desired color and position them at equal spacing at the bottom of your table. Screw firmly into place.

✓ Check for any rough places, and your new table is ready for use!

4. Practical Pallet Chair

What you need:

- Pallets
- Hammer
- Nails
- Stain
- Saw
- Pencil
- Measuring tape

How to make it:

- ✓ Begin by dismantling the pallet completely. You might need two, so disassemble two.

- ✓ You will need 16 2 foot long planks, which you should cut. You'll also need four 4 foot boards, two 3 foot boards (cut with their legs at an angle to lay on the floor), and one support board.

- ✓ Sand them all smooth and arrange them. Screw all 16 boards at an angle, these are the seat of the chair, then screw both sets of 4-foot-long boards at right angles, then consult the photo again to determine where to position the chair's feet.

- ✓ Screw the entire piece together, and apply a stain. Let dry, and use a cushion over the top.

5. Rustic Indoor Pallet Table

What you need:

- 1 pallet
- Saw
- 2-by-4 post
- Hammer
- Hand drill
- 7/8-inch self-tapping metal threaded screws
- 6-inch pipe flange
- 6-inch pipe
- 6-inch pipe coupler
- Wood tabletop
- Tablecloth

How to make it:

✓ A pallet should be examined to learn about its manufacture. Any nails should be taken off. In the alternative, you might lay the pallet flat and begin sawing the boards.

✓ You should measure the size of your dining table in your home and deduct the leg thickness to determine the height of the pallet tabletop.

✓ The pipe table legs' dimensions may now be measured. To match the height of the tables, they are also modified. Cut a pallet board, fix it to the pipe, and mark the location of the pipe hole.

✓ Drill the spot, and then screw in a metal screw with a 7/8-inch thread. The pipe was now removed in accordance with the desired tabletop's needed dimensions.

✓ The planks may be fixed in place once the tabletop has been placed by inserting the 7/8-inch threaded metal screw into the pipe that runs through their bottoms.

✓ For the remaining pipe setting and tabletop setup, repeat the previous stages.

✓ Using a drill and 7/8-inch self-tapping metal threaded screws, you must secure a 6-inch pipe flange to the table legs.

✓ To gauge the height of the table legs, you need attach a 6-inch pipe using a pipe coupler.

✓ The pipe and flange at the base of the table may be concealed using the tablecloth.

6. Pallet Bookshelf

What you need:

- 4 white painted pallets
- Sandpaper
- Lumber (any)
- Wood Glue
- Wood filler
- Clamps
- Paint
- Screwdriver
- Router
- Cordless drill
- Back Brackets
- MDF or hardwood plywood
- 3/4 inch large wood screw
- Cabinets handles
- Dovetail bits

How to make it:

- ✓ You should clean every pallet before doing anything to get rid of unnecessary items. If they have a lot of stickers, you can apply them.

- ✓ You can see nails on the inside, therefore a rope made of several nails might be used to clean the pallets.

✓ You must now transport them to the workshop so that the top coat of our pallets may be removed. Check for any undesired materials by sanding the top.

✓ Now you must cut the lumber to create the sides. For each side, you can use 5 or 6 pieces of timber.

✓ Make sure the lengths of the sides are equal.

✓ Using wood glue and clamps to dry, secure the pallet sides in their proper locations.

✓ You must glue and cut the lumber to create the bottom tier of our pallet bookshelf. For the bottom layer, cut hardwood plywood pieces that are the same length and width as our pallet.

✓ Now use a router and trim the bottom layer's circular edge. You must make sure that the router bit does not touch the pallets' sides.

✓ The bottom layer must be painted with brown or any darker color.

✓ By inserting a 3/4-inch wood screw into the pallet's reverse side, dowels are created. These dowels are easily fixed in the pallets' sides.

✓ Now, place the bottom layer that you painted in the centre of the 88 pallets, with 8 pallets serving as edge pieces.

✓ Now drill three 3/4-inch holes into the bottom layer's interpallets.

✓ Pallets should have the back brackets installed and the dowels inserted into the holes.

✓ Cut the pallet bookshelf's drawers. Pallets may easily be converted into drawers.

✓ They should be painted a pale brown tone.

7. Piping Desk

What do you need:

- 1 x EMT 70-inch conduit
- EMT conduit 4 x 30-inch
- 2 x 16-inch conduit for EMT
- Six x T-connectors
- 4 x plugs with ends
- 4 x 3⁄4-inch floor flanges for the pipe
- Screws from timber
- Wooden desktop 98-inch

How to make it:

✓ To build the frame, attach a T-connector to each edge of the 70-inch EMT pipe and tighten it using the included tools.

✓ Calculate and identify the 16-inch conduits' middles. Fill each T-connector with a 16-inch EMT conduit until the center T-connector reaches the desired location.

✓ Remaining T-connectors should be attached to the 16-inch conduits' margins. With the Allen wrench, position the connection so that the opening ends are vertical.

✓ Each 30-inch pipe should be valued and labeled six inches from the rim. Before the midpoint of the vertically oriented T-connectors lines up with the label, float the 30-inch sections one at a time through them. To fasten the connections to the pipe, use the Allen wrench and the included hardware.

✓ Turn the desktop so that it is facing downward. To verify that the frame is balanced, flip the pipe upside-down frame so that the flanges are on the bottom of the desktop.

✓ Calculate the distance from the desktop side to the flanges on each side of the block, then mark the center of each hole within each flange.

✓ Make pilot holes in the desktop surrounding each connecting hole. It is crucial to take this action in order to keep the wood from shattering. Once the pilot holes are made, insert the wood screws. Once you've turned your desk in the proper way, you're done.

Home Accessories

8. DIY Wood Doormat

What you need:

- two – 1×4 cedar boards
- table saw
- miter box
- nail gun (or hammer & nails)
- wood glue
- sandpaper

How to make it:

✓ Split 1 to 4 by half with the table saw. Cut a slice of your frame cedar board thickness (we were at 13/16). Measure and decide the duration of your 13/16).

✓ Measure and decide the duration of your degree angles on either end of the frame pieces by using the miter box. Clue the frame and weld it together. Cut the board at an angle of 45 degrees, place the corner part firmly on your side, and mark the other end you have to cut.

✓ Break the piece inside the frame in another 45-degree angle, glue and nail it. Repeat until the frame is complete. (We used two small pieces of wood just to maintain the distance between the boards). Clean the sides and the boards between them.

9. Wooden Vase

What do you need:

- Wood twigs of different sizes
- Steel can
- Saw
- Glue
- Sandpaper

How to make it:

✓ The first thing you actually need to do is gather some nearby, conveniently accessible wood twigs.

✓ Reduce the size of the twigs. To create these little, aesthetically pleasing objects, use twigs of various diameters.

✓ Sandpaper should now be used to smooth the surfaces of the cut ends of the twig pieces.

✓ Take the steel container and clean it thoroughly to remove any residue.

✓ Now begin using the adhesive to attach each piece of the cut wood, one at a time. Start attaching these pieces from the bottom and move them upward.

✓ Your lovely wooden vase is now prepared for exhibition. It may be placed on a table in your kitchen, living room, study, or even dining room.

10. Hexagon Shelves

What do you need:

- Wood, 1-inch x 4-inch or 6-inch x 6-foot
- Miter saw (one may also obtain the timber cut for himself at the hardware store)
- Sandpaper
- Glue for wood
- Gun Staple
- Minwax Wood Organic finish
- Brush Sponge
- Acrylic paint yellow

How to make it:

✓ If you are cutting the wood by hand, start by setting your miter saw to 30° and cutting six 8-inch pieces of wood, making sure that only the cuts from both scales are pointed inward (see image above).

✓ Next, construct the hexagon and adhere the wood glue to all of the joints. Give it an hour to dry.

✓ Staple each conjunction and the two stitches on the back of the hexagon after turning it over. Allow it to dry for 24 hours.

✓ After they have dried, sand a few rough corners.

✓ The time to customise is right now. On the outside, we dyed a natural skin tone, and within, we painted yellow. Let it dry only.

✓ The corners of each hexagon will be covered with nails, or mount each rack with a bracket.

11. Super Slim End Table

What you need:

- Pallets
- Saw
- Hammer
- Stain
- Nails

How to make it:

✓ Simply cut 1 pallet down the center of each of the support pieces. Sand down and apply a stain, then stack up as you see in the photo.

✓ Apply another stain, and screw in place. Let dry, and you are done!

12. Mini Desk Masterpiece

What you need:

- Pallets
- Hammer
- Nails
- Stain
- Saw
- Sandpaper
- Pencil
- Measuring tape

How to make it:

✓ Begin by removing all of the wood from one side of the pallet. Mark on your pallet where you need to cut and measure your desk where the stand will go. Follow these lines with your saw, then sand the wood smooth using sandpaper.

✓ Stain the wood now to bring out the natural appearance.

✓ Sand down any remaining rough parts, and your stand is complete!

13.   Crazy Mandala Paint Piece

What do you need:

- 9 mm circle cutter
- 24-inch ruler
- Sponge paintbrush
- 12 inches by 12 inches watercolor paper
- White matte spray
- Gray grout

How to make it:

✓ The first mark should be made one inch from the bottom using a 24-inch ruler. Make sure you mark 4 inches on either side of the center and repeat the process for the remaining 3 inches.

✓ To cut out the circles, program the circle cutter. Apply it to paper that is 1/4 inch thick.

✓ You must now center the line on one of the circles using the 2 mm line you selected on the circle cutter. Press firmly when placing the circle cutter over the circle. The 9 mm circular ought should be simple to cut out.

✓ Keeping this circle still, trace it from below on the paper. Repeat the process with additional rings after the water has dried up.

✓ Apply white matte spray on the object.

✓ Fill a container with the grout and water mixture. Utilizing a flat-edged utensil, stir the mixture until the water turns clear. Use the flat-edged instrument to spread the mixture over the artwork while keeping it in a plastic container. The paint will lace out of the grout mixture as you run the tool to mix the grout and paint. Swirl and rub the tool in opposite directions to create a textured pattern.

14.   Wood Doormat

What do you need:

- Square End Balusters 8 -36" x 2" x 2"
- 1-Sisal Rope Natural
- Stain Wood (Brown and Colored)
- Paintbrush
- Tools:
- Circular Saw
- Drill
- Box Cutter
- Tape Measurement
- Pencil
- Block Sanding
- Painters Tape
- Gloves
- Headgear

How to make it:

- ✓ Use a prepared tape measure and a pencil to count and then cut the wood in the quarter. You will receive 16, 18 balusters.

- ✓ All (16) 18" long pieces have holes drilled on both ends, 1" from the edge, using your machine and a 3/8" drill bit.

- ✓ The slice's angular surfaces should be sanded.

- ✓ Stain every component of your 18" (we used Dark Walnut from Minmax)

- ✓ a box cutter to cut two 80-inch-long sisal string strips

- ✓ We taped off each 18-inch baluster for parts 3-6 inches wide, making sure to do so on a baluster outside the area and on the closest piece of wood inside the section. So we painted the 6" pieces with the colored wood finish (weather resistant).

- ✓ Secure a knot at the bottom of one of the 80" long rope pieces as a very final step. Loop the other end of the rope into the gap between two pieces of the crown molding and tie a knot. Begin sewing through the holes. Tie a knot when you reach the top.

15. Plant Stand

What do you need:

- Hardwood dowel of 3/4" (red oak, walnut, rosewood, teak, etc.)
- Hardwood timber one 1/2" x 3/4" (same wood type as dowel)
- Dowels of 1/8"
- Glue for wood
- The organic finish of wood (Minwax, etc.)
- Push Drill
- Forstner Bit 3/4"
- Panel Saw (can be done with a jigsaw)
- Clamps Over
- Palm sander orbital (optional)
- Fine sandpaper of grit

How to make it:

- ✓ For the straps, create two 1 1/2" x 3/4" portions that are broader than the pot's diameter. (We applied 9 "to complement our West Elm planter)

- ✓ Cut a 3/4" x 3/4" scratch on the table saw (with a miter jig or sled) or with a jigsaw at the halfway point of each length.

- ✓ Perhaps not truly useable in this fashion, portable drill, clamp each crossbar, and grind out each end halfway through the Forstner bit through and the drill press (the only bit that might create incomplete holes are Forstner bits, but the workpiece should be firmly secured).

✓ Cross each side of the middle crossbars with 1/8" holes that are 1/2" deep (for 1/8 "dowels)

✓ Cut four pieces of 3/4" dowels to the required height for the plant stand (mine was 18").

✓ Drill 1/8" holes in each 3/4" dowel where the pot base should be. "For the best centering results, utilize a self-centering drill press jig" (we used the midway point here).

✓ If it is, make the necessary adjustments on a belt sander for leveling. For a coarse paper, notches in the crossbars may be extended or go back to the table saw or jigsaw. To ensure it fits, join both pieces together with dowels and make sure the stand is straight.

✓ When everything fuses firmly and smoothly, sand each component flawlessly.

✓ Put wood glue in each joint and dowel hole, securely fasten everything, and let it sit for 6–12 hours.

✓ Use the wooden finish alternative to secure and finish the end product.

Outdoor Accessories

16.   Rustic Pallet Wagon

What you need:

- Pallets
- Hammer
- Nails
- Stain
- Saw
- Pencil
- Measuring tape
- Wheels
- Rope

How to make it:

✓ Begin by sanding your pallet. There should be no rough spots or possibly slivers of wood. Use a stain.

✓ Once the stay has dried, flip the pallet over and mark the location of the wheels with a pencil. Screw them firmly into place.

✓ For the handle, I propose purchasing two hooks from your local hardware shop and screwing them into the wagon's front. Tie the rope tightly via these hooks. That's all! Your wagon is prepared for any situation.

17. DIY Coffee Table

What you need:

- Drill
- Hot glue gun
- Paint or stain
- Chest or suitcase
- Staple gun
- Measuring tape
- Legs and Storage containers
- Top plate hardware
- Velvet or fabric
- Wallpaper
- Cording or trim
- Wooden dividers

How to make it:

✓ Sand the pallet woods and then paint them to complement the colors of your chest. Carefully examine the chest and remove any torn fabric to give a neat look to your coffee table storage.

✓ Measure the legs and then prepare all four legs to secure them at a right place. You can use a machine gun to fix nails and use wooden dividers to make small compartments. It will be good to decorate your wooden dividers with wallpaper.

18.   Storage Shed for Garden

What you need:

- Tape Measure
- 1 board of 24 feet, 2 x 4 inch
- Flour
- 6 Reber of 4 foot
- Jig saw
- Rubber mallet
- Hammer
- 3 lengths of 14 PVC pipe, ¾ inch and 12 feet long
- Polyethylene 12 x 2 feet plastic
- Nails
- Fencing staples
- Wire

How to make it:

- ✓ Determine the size of your portable garage. You must use flour to indicate this specific location. The garage should be 6 feet long and 4 feet broad.

- ✓ With the rubber mallet, smash the Rebar supports halfway into the floor at each corner of the garage. Hammer the remaining supports halfway into the ground on either side of the shed.

✓ Curve each piece of PVC to form a U shape, and keep the arm of each U at the end of the Rebar support glued out of the floor.

✓ Drape a wire all the way around the curve of the first PVC pipe section. Run a wire loosely through the second length of pipe and drape it. You may stretch the wire all the way to the end of the pipe and drape it freely. You can build a ridge post that can withstand the weight of snow.

✓ Now, cut the board into two 6-foot pieces and one 4-foot piece. To build an open square, you'll need more wood. You can maintain this square at the bottom of the garage frame's outside Rebar surface and leave one side open.

✓ It's time to draw the polyethylene shell at the garage border's apex to maintain one side flush with the garage's façade. You may secure it using fence tacks. It's time to let a back lynching hang free so that the wind may blow from the front to the actual back and the rain doesn't come as hard.

19.   Shelves for Garden

What you need:

- Sandpaper
- Drill, Level, and Hammer
- 2 wood pallets
- Wood screws
- Wood, 2 by 4 inches
- Saw and Nails
- Paint and Paintbrush
- Wall anchors

How to make it:

✓ To get pallets with a smooth surface, you must really sand the wood's surface in the initial stage. Each pallet's bottom can be used.

✓ The pallets will be joined together using drills and wood screws. Maintain one pallet on top of each pallet facing the same way. The shelves will be grabbed by the undersides.

✓ Measure the actual width of the inside of the top pallet and cut the wood to 2 by 4 inches. Insert this wood horizontally into the pallet, keeping it 6 to 8 inches from the top of the wood. Before keeping it on top of the wood, check the level of the wood to ensure it is even. Use a hammer and nails to secure the shelf. Repeat the process for each shelf.

✓ To get a rustic aesthetic, paint your shelves or leave them untreated. You may secure the shelf unit to the wall using wall studs or anchors.

20.   Playhouse in Patio

What you need:

- 1 sheet 1/2-inch pallet wood, 8 feet x 4 feet
- Circular saw and Hammer
- Tape measure
- Straight edge
- 2-inch galvanized nails
- Pencil
- Construction adhesive
- 21 x 34 inches for bottom
- 27 x 39 inches for top
- 23 x 24 inches for back
- 23 x 24 inches for front
- 24 x 34 inches for side
- 24 x 34 inches for another side

How to make it:

✓ Cut the pieces of pallet wood boards for the following measurements:

✓ You have to create a door at the bottom edge of the front piece, but mark it with a pencil. You can cut out the rectangle or round door.

✓ Line up the back panel and the panels on both the sides and fix with nail and hammer along the length of the panels. Now secure the front panel with hammering electrified nails.

✓ It is time to set the wooden frame on the top of the bottom piece and fix it with two to three nails on each corner. Keep a flat panel in its place with hammer and nails and keep it secure. Add adhesive constructions and let the pet house dry.

21. Pallet Garden Sofa

What you need:

- 9 Pallets
- Drill, Level, and Hammer
- Sandpaper
- Saw and Nails
- Paint and Paintbrush
- Wood screws

How to make it:

✓ Collect Your Pallet. The average size of pallet will be 9 and you should select the best quality pallets to design sofa. You can find some cool wood burned or stamped wood. It is important to check a few extra details.

✓ Cut Pallets. You have to cut these pallets at 27.5 inches wide to mix and match them easily. You can cut right directly across the planks and remove a few edges on the side 2 by 4. You can reuse 2 by 4 by sliding it into the space and reattach with the help of nails. The overall length can be 78"x 78".

✓ Create Cushions. You have to hide front 2 by 4 gap of the pallet with cushions and mattresses. You can use a few mattresses to create your own cushion because the foam can be expensive and you can cut an old mattress to make cushions.

✓ Secure Backs. You can use a few screws to overlap pallets and screw them along the seam. It will be good to use 2-inch screws. You can decorate your patio and use in parties for extra sitting arrangements.

22.   DIY Garden Chair

What you need:

- Miter saw
- Flat bar
- 2 wooden pallets
- Nail puller
- Box, stainless steel screws
- Measurement tape
- Screw gun

How to make it:

✓ Take a wooden pallet and keep it flat on the work surface with the peak surface facing up. The flat bar will slide under the first two boards at one end of the pallet and snoop them carefully.

✓ Pull out the nails of every pallet board with the help of nail puller. Clean the pallets by removing any drifted nails and set the boards on one side. Repeat this process and remove the nails from each board and cut the pallet boards for the back of the chair, legs and arms.

✓ Take two boards and measure the 12-inch surface with the help of measure tape and pencil. Use miter saw and cut to the length of the front leg.

✓ Place the end, conflicting the detached boards, on the chair assembly pallet and move it in an upward direction. Keep one forward-facing support on each side at the elevated end and drive four wood screws with equal space through the leg into the exterior of the pallet with the use of screw gun.

✓ Put the second pallet level on the surface while keeping the top surface in an upward direction. Remove half board from one end of the pallet and clean it by pulling the nails out with the help of nail puller. This pallet will help you to assemble seat and ends with the removal of boards for back legs.

✓ Insert the pallet designed for a back seat with the back leg down through the fourth board. Bring down the back legs on the work surface and used four screws to fasten the seat. You can use a screw gun to fix the each joint of the chair.

23. Pallet Stool for Garden

What you need:

- 4 pieces of wood to make the legs of the stool (3 inches thick)
- Drill and wood glue
- 4 inch thick wood for seat
- Chisel
- 4 large screws
- Varnish
- Padding and upholstery

How to make it:

✓ Measure the stool as per your needs and then select pallet wood to make the stool. Cut into different pieces of the wood to make legs and seat. The seat can be round or square.

✓ Drill holes in the seat to fix legs in the four corners, you need to insert screws into each of the four corners on the bar stool. Cut down the legs to determine the height of your stool and try to keep these pieces 3 inches thick. Make sure to keep the size of all four legs same.

✓ You can use wood glue in the holes of the seat around the screw head and carefully insert the legs into the hole. Screw them until you get resistance and make sure to keep it tight. Clean the excessive glue and let the stool dry.

24.   Pallet Bin for Compost and Plants

What you need:

- 8-foot pieces of 1 x 4 pine, 2 boards
- 10-foot pieces of 1 x 2 pine, 2 boards
- 10-foot piece of 2 x 2 pine, 1 board
- Measuring tape and Clamp
- Safety goggles
- Circular saw
- 1 box of about 1 1/4-inch screws
- Drill and 7/16 drill bit

How to make it:

✓ Use a circular saw to cut all of the wooden parts, such as 4 pieces of 24-inch 1 x 4, 4 pieces of 22 inches, and 4 pieces of 2 x 2 at 30 inches. You will also need to cut four 1 x 2 pieces at 24 inches and six 25-inch sections.

✓ You will need to construct four walls, two of which will be constructed with 22-inch 1 x 4 pieces and two of which will be constructed with 24-inch 1 x 4 pieces. You will construct the corners by constructing square walls. Fasten them together and put the top and bottom together.

✓ To secure each rack, drill a screw into each part of the inner rack. Complete the bottom portion, then similarly get ready the top portion. To protect the rack, you might apply paint or sealer.

25. Outdoor Bench

What do you need:

- 12 cinder blocks (we used these Home Depot 8"x8"x16" cinder blocks at $1.58 each)
- "4-4"x4"x8" bits of wood (we obtained these from Lowe's)
- Waterseal by Thompson
- Nails Oil

How to make it:

✓ We trimmed each 4x4 to a length of 7 since eight was too long for a bench width in the space we were utilizing.

✓ We applied Thompson's Water Seal on the wood to protect it from the elements. Although you are free to choose to paint the wood, we like the way the raw wood looked.

✓ The project's most time-consuming step was leveling the area where we placed the bench. We put in a lot of shoveling time and effort to get it perfect.

✓ Once it was finished, we decided where the 12 blocks would be placed (6 on each side, with four standing upright vertically and 2 stacked on top of them horizontally).

✓ Before inserting the 4x4s into the top 4 holes, we conformed the blocks with liquid nails for additional structural support because they are sturdy and didn't seem to move.

26.   Rack to Keep Your Tools

What you need:

- 1 pallet
- Staples
- 4′ x 4′ chicken wire
- 6 wire coat hangers
- Durable chain
- 2 1/4 x 4″ clasp hook bolts and nuts
- 4 washers with bolts
- S-shaped hooks
- Circular Saw and Hammer
- Nail Puller and Nails
- Drill and head screwdriver
- Staple gun and wire cutters
- Tape to Measure

How to make it:

✓ Cut the pallets and remove the middle bar of the pallet. Carefully split the wood and measure the split pieces. You should use a staple gun to staple the chicken wire in a particular place. Staple the chicken wire to the wooden bar.

✓ Cut the additional wire with the help of a wire cutter and bend the remaining wire to make the sharp corners smooth. Take the wooden bars and fix the chicken wire with the help of screws and use a nail gun to fix the wood pallets.

✓ Fix the chain along the length and hang the rack at about a 45-degree angle with hook bolts on the wall. Your pot rack is ready and now you can use bolts to fix the rack at a point where you can access it and create additional support.

✓ You can place S-hooks on the hanger wire so that you can hang pots and pans on the hooks. Keep it in mind that these hooks can carry a lightweight item, but you can get the benefits of additional storage.

27.   Hanging Garden

What do you need:

- Flower pots
- Rope
- 3/4" Pine Boards
- Zip Ties
- Drill
- Saw (preferably whole saw)
- Pliers
- Paint (if needed)

How to make it:

✓ The pine planks must first be trimmed to the correct length.

✓ Now, drill a hole through the wood planks.

✓ To mark the place for the hole, use a pencil. Make careful you allow a space of 2 inches between the pots and 1 inch between the rope and the board corner.

✓ Place every board in a pile, then begin poking holes in every board at once. Drill a pilot hole first to serve as a reference point for the saw blade to subsequently cut.

✓ Now, take each board and use a saw to cut the holes, using the pilot holes as a guide.

✓ Create holes for the rope at each of the board's four corners now. Make sure they are large enough for the rope to pass through.

✓ Apply the same procedure to all the boards.

✓ Now smoothen the boards by rubbing them with sandpaper.

✓ If you actually wish to, you can also use your own preferred paint.

✓ Now thread the rope through the gaps in the boards' corners and secure it with a knot at the base.

✓ Now line the rope coming from each board with the others.

✓ You may now hang your hanging garden wherever you wish to exhibit it. check to see whether it can support the weight of the boards and pots.

✓ Zip ties are required to maintain a sufficient distance between the plants. Place the boards in the proper position, wrap the zip tie over it, and then tighten it. Now use pliers to trim the superfluous portion. Use two or three zip ties for each area to further fasten.

✓ Fill the holes with flower pots.

28. Garden Bench

What do you need:

- 5 pieces of lumber (2 x 4 x 8 ft)
- 1 piece of lumber (1 x 4 x 4 ft)
- 1 piece of lumber (4 x 4 x 8 ft)
- 2 threaded rod (3/8-in.-dia x 36-in.)
- 4 of each hex nuts and washers (3/8-in.). The outside diameter should be 9/16 in.
- Polyurethane glue
- 1 wooden dowel (1-in.-dia.)
- 1 box decking screws (1 5/8-in.)
- 1 box galvanized finishing nails (1 1/2-in. (4d))

How to make it:

- ✓ Use a circular/power mister saw and a crosscut guide then cut 4 legs, 12 spacers to length and 9 seat boards.

- ✓ Start to flip the legs over then make a second shoulder cut. Pare to perfection by the use of a razor-sharp chisel.

- ✓ Pin to six 2in × 4in seat panels blocks 3 ½ inches square and ¾ inches thick as insertions. By the use of a 1 ½ inch 4 diameter finishing nails and glue fasten the block with outer edge on ends.

- ✓ on the 2 outer seat boards for the counter bored holes mark center points for the rods and nuts that hold the seat together. Now, drill a ¾-inch- hole with 1-inch-diameter. The wood plug will be received by the counter bored holes and they will eliminate the hex nuts on the ends of the rods that are threaded.

- ✓ Make a plywood dance and screw it onto a guide for you to be able to drill the 7/16-inch-diameter holes for the rods. This will make sure that any hole complete each piece is precisely located relative to the panel's end. Then try to hold the jig to be alongside the end of each seat panel before boring through the panel and spacer block.

- ✓ On a workbench glue and clamp all the fragments together and cut the threaded pole to have a measurement of nineteen inches. Onto the end of each rod thread a nut, eliminate the nut for you to clean up any saw damage.

- ✓ Place a nut and washer at the ends of each pole then with a 9/16-inch socket ratchet it fitted.

- ✓ Use 80- or 100-grit sandpaper to respectively even surfaces then use a clean brush to remove any sanding dust.

29.　Camp Kitchen

What do you need:

- 1 Bottom – 32-1/2" x 14 X 1/2"
- 2 Sides --19" x 14" x 1/2"
- 1 Divider -- 18- 1/2" x 14" x 1/2"
- 1 Shelf -- 20" x 14 x1/2"
- 1 Top -- 12" x 14" x 1/2"
- 1 Top Leaf, Right -- 12-1/2" x 14-1/4" x1/2"
- 1 Top Leaf, Left – 20-7/8" x 14-1/4" x1/2"
- 1 Door, Left –12 ¾"x 20" x ½"
- 1 Door, Right --18"x12"x ½"
- 1 Back – ¾"- ½"" x 19" x ¼"
- Base (made of hardwood)
- 2 pieces 31-1/2" x 3/4"
- 2 Pieces -- 12" x 3/4"
- 4 Legs -- 1" x 1" x12"
- 2 Pieces Stop Molding 3/4" x3/8" for Door Stops
- Hardware
- 4 Pairs, butt hinges 1" x 2" or piano hinge
- 2 Door knobs
- 2 Roller Catches
- 2 Folding Trays for the Top Leafs
- 1/4 lb. 1- 1/2" finishing nails

- Glue
- 4 Carriage Bolts complete with Washers and Wing Nuts -- 2" x 1/4"
- 1 Pint Marine or Outdoor Quality Paint

How to make it:

✓ You will need approximately 1 sheet of 4' x 8' x 1/2 "plywood (no more).

✓ Cut all pieces to the sizes given on your material list.

✓ Using glue on every joint, begin by nailing both sides against the ends of the bottom.

✓ Next measure 5-1/4" down from the top on both your left side and the divider and nail the shelf in place, the top (right) comes next and the divider is then nailed onto the bottom.

✓ Every piece must be square-cut, of course, and, with the back glued and nailed will stiffen the whole cabinet.

✓ Doors and top leafs are fitted next and, using either butt or piano hinges, screwed into place.

✓ Stop molding is nailed to the divider and roller catches fastened to them to hold the doors secure. Install door knobs and leaf stays last.

✓ Both leafs must be mortised to accept the stays when the top is open. Take care to install the stays so that the leafs stand out square to the cabinet sides.

✓ The interior arrangement is subject to personal preference and should be made to accept your existing gear.

✓ See the model photo #1 below

✓ The small divider on the right side must be large enough to accept a gasoline can.

✓ A camp lantern, either single or double burner, will fit next to it and is held in place by 2 screw eyes or hooks and a rubber band to prevent it from rattling.

✓ On the left an extra shelf can be installed to accept camp griddle or other miscellaneous items.

✓ A dishpan with nesting cook and dinnerware is held in place by a small wooden molding and again hooks and rubber band.

✓ Cutlery, openers etc., will fit into another small divider.

✓ The base is cut from hardwood and can be glued and nailed, with the end pieces fitting between the long pieces.

✓ The legs are bolted, one bolt to each leg, but care must be taken that they will fold completely inside the base and when you are folding them out. They must be close enough to the outside of the base so that they cannot fold out further than about 10 degrees.

✓ The wing nuts will allow you to tighten the bolts so that the legs cannot fold accidently but are still somewhat adjustable.

30.   Pallet Bin for Compost and Plants

What do you need:

- 8-foot pieces of 1 x 4 pine, 2 boards
- 10-foot pieces of 1 x 2 pine, 2 boards
- 10-foot piece of 2 x 2 pine, 1 board
- Measuring tape and Clamp
- Safety goggles
- Circular saw
- 1 box of about 1 1/4-inch screws
- Drill and 7/16 drill bit

How to make it:

✓ Cut all the wooden pieces with the help of a circular saw, such as you need 4 pieces of 24-inch of 1 x 4, 4 pieces of 22 inches, and 4 pieces of 2 x 2 at 30 inches. You will also cut 4 pieces of 1 x 2 at 24 inches and 6 pieces of 25 inches.

✓ You need to build four walls, two walls will be built by 22-inch piece of 1 x 4 and two walls can be designed with 24-inch one x four pieces. You will make square walls build the corners. Fasten them together and assemble the top and bottom area.

✓ Cut the sections for inner rack and drill a screw in each rack to fix it. Finish off the bottom part and prepare the top part in the same way. You can add sealant or paint to protect the rack.

31. Grow Your Herbal Garden

What do you need:

- Wall adhesive
- Tapcon screws
- Wooden pallet
- Hose clamps
- Mason jars
- Soil
- Cable Staples
- Charcoal
- Stones
- Plants

How to make it:

✓ Use a wood that will serve as a base for the wall and place hose clamps on this wooden board. You can measure the place on a wooden board to find out the capacity of glass jars on the wooden board. If you want to grow herbs, these should be located close to your window. You can grow sage, rosemary, and similar herbs.

✓ After securing the boards in its place, you can use adhesive to secure the board and use tap con screw to make it secure in its place. Now you will measure the center to fix the hose clamps and secure them in their right place.

✓ Pour stones in the bottom of mason jars and make sure these should be free from drainage. After stones, you can add charcoal to balance the pH of soil and avoid growth of bacteria in soil. Now add soil and plants in every jar and secure them with the hose clamps.

Chapter 4: Mistakes and How to Avoid Them

Slowing down

When you're attempting to build a woodworking project, you should be aware of common mistakes that can cost you time and money. These mistakes usually result from poor planning and attention to detail, but there are a few steps you can take to avoid them. First, don't try to take on complicated projects before you have mastered the basics.

Taking accurate measurements is essential for the success of any woodworking project. Even the slightest measurement error can affect the finished product. Incorrect measurements can lead to loose joints, unwanted spaces, and overlaps. Make sure to make accurate measurements of every piece of wood to ensure that your project turns out perfectly.

Another common mistake involves the use of the wrong tool. Sometimes, you may accidentally insert a screw or nail into a piece of wood and cause a split. To repair a split, use glue and wax paper to secure the split piece of wood. After this, wait for it to dry.

Using a router

When using a router, beginners should always make sure that they are using the correct bit for the job. While this may seem obvious, the wrong router bit can actually cause damage to your woodworking project. The wrong bit can damage the wood as well as impede the precision of the router. To avoid this, beginners should make sure that they clean their router bits after each use. Resins and dust can build up on the surface of the router bit and create resistance. This will make it difficult to make smooth edges and will result in rough edges.

When using a router to cut wood, it is important to avoid cutting too thin a piece. It is best to use thick wood that gives enough depth to your cuts. You can also use various router bits to achieve decorative edges. If you do not have a lot of experience, you can watch a tutorial online to learn how to use a router and avoid common mistakes.

Using a router can make a lot of projects easier. You can use it to cut long pieces of wood and create intricate designs with grooves and holes. It can also be used for carving and imitating sculpture. Its versatility makes it a good tool for beginners.

Using a miter gauge

One of the first steps to making accurate cuts with a miter gauge is to use a miter gauge. A miter gauge is a tool used to determine the angle of cuts. The miter head on the gauge rotates around a central point and is often clamped in place with a push handle. The miter gauge head has preset stops for making adjustments.

To check if the miter gauge is working properly, use a piece of wood at least five inches wide and several feet long. Make sure the board has parallel sides. Then, place the board on the miter gauge and cut along the marked line. When you are done, you should hold the board against the table and ensure that the edges are flat.

Before using a miter gauge, you should be sure to read the instructions on the guide bar. The bar should fit the slot snugly without any side-to-side movement. When the miter gauge does not fit properly, you will run the risk of a jam or accident. To ensure the best fit, woodworking supply houses carry UHMW tape, which acts as a spacer between the miter gauge and the slot.

Using a router table

A router table is the most popular shop tool in the world. However, new users may run into a few problems. For example, they may not install the base plate properly. This may result in a cut that is not as precise as they would have liked. A base plate is a necessity, as it ensures that the cutting bit sits in the center of the table. Also, clams can help stabilize the object or workpiece, which will ensure better precision.

Using a router table correctly is essential for achieving good results. While the bits on a router table are relatively small, they can cause serious injury if not used correctly. This is why you should wear protective eyewear and ear protection while using your router table. In addition, you should use a featherboard to support large pieces of stock. Another good idea is to use push blocks to keep your hands away from the bits.

Router tables come in two main types: benchtop and floorstanding. Benchtop router tables are typically smaller and compact. Some can fold down for storage when not in use. Floor standing router tables, on the other hand, are usually large and heavy. They also cannot be moved easily. To choose a table, first decide on the type of workpiece you plan to work on.

Using a jig

Using a jig to cut out pieces is an easy way to ensure proper measurements for your projects and avoid common woodworking mistakes. For example, when making drawer fronts, a jig can help you ensure the exact dimensions of your workpiece. This will save you time, frustration, and money. A jig can also help you avoid mistakes like burnt edges.

Using the wrong blade for the job is another common mistake that woodworkers make. It is essential to select the correct blade for the type of project that you are working on, so that you don't end up with an ugly cut or a lot of tearout.

Using the wrong tool is also a common mistake in woodworking. Not only is the wrong tool expensive, it also leaves the wood unaligned, which is a big problem. When preparing for a project, use a level to check for straightness and a moisture meter to ensure that the wood is not too dry.

Another common mistake in woodworking is not leaving enough space for wood to expand or contract. If the wood is not allowed to acclimate properly, it will warp, bow, and warp. A jig helps you avoid these common mistakes by allowing your wood to expand or contract before you attach it to a project.

Using a planer

Using a planer can be tricky and can cost you time and money. However, it's important to use the right tools to get the job done. One of the most common mistakes is misaligning the wood with the tool. This can result in uneven wood surfaces. To avoid this, you should use a level and a moisture meter to check the wood for straightness.

Another mistake beginners make is not clearing the work area of obstructions before using the planer. This can lead to tearing out the grain or losing tiny chunks of wood. Using a planer correctly will make the wood look more uniform and will lead to fewer mistakes.

A planer is easier to use than a sander, but it does take practice to get the job done right. Sandpaper, on the other hand, is more difficult to control, and it requires a lot of trial and error to get the right results. A sander can remove too much material, so it is vital to use it carefully.

Dents in wood can be easily repaired, but the wood can't always be flat. It's important to remember that they can occur anywhere on the wood. It can also occur due to improper angles. Thankfully, these mistakes are easily rectified. For softwoods, you can use water to dampen the wood before applying pressure to it. However, if you're working with hardwoods, you may need to use an electric clothes iron to smooth out the dent.

Using a jointer

If you're using a jointer to cut wood, here are some common mistakes to avoid. First, make sure your infeed and outfeed tables are parallel. This will help you produce a square edge. Secondly, make sure the fence stops are adjusted correctly. A slight bow or crown should not affect accuracy, but a fence that is warped or twisted will make it difficult to joint a square edge.

Another common mistake is using a jointer to cut too deeply. The best rule of thumb is to make one-sixteenth-inch cuts. This will prevent kickbacks. You should also make sure your jointer is locked. If it is not, you may be exposing the blade to a dangerously sharp object.

In addition to cutting lumber properly, you should also take note of the way the workpiece is finished. A jointer can make a smooth surface of a piece, but it should never be cut through end grain. You should also surface the concave side of a warped board first. Also, make sure that the floor around the jointer is clean.

As a beginner, using a jointer can be frustrating. It's difficult to get a perfect board with a jointer unless you know how to use a table saw and a wood planer. It's not possible to achieve the perfect board with a jointer, but a bench jointer can quickly flatten a board.

Conclusion

Some kits are for beginners with little carpentry or building experience, but they take the time to follow the directions for safety. These storage building children are also a lot cheaper than buying an existing shed. If you don't want to bring the package together yourself, you should sometimes buy it, and the manufacturer pays an extra cost for the kit. Depending on how you choose to do the assembly, you will remember a few things: which material to use-wood, acrylic, steel, plastic, etc. Vinyl sets are the lowest maintenance and long-lasting yet expensive.

Wood kits can be mounted in a landscape that complements the yard or the garden. Steel and steel sheds fit very well for large storage requirements. They are sturdy and strong, but they can rust over time. The simpler the instructions, the more illustrations and photos used to display assembly steps, the more straightforward the kit is to be assembled.

CONCLUSION

Woodworking can be an extremely satisfying and possibly even life-changing interest! But being good at woodworking doesn't come naturally to everyone. As stated earlier, woodworking involves some form of advanced technology and techniques that must be diligently taught and adopted with time and dedication to be made. The time spent studying and practising proper craftsmanship should yield impressive positive results.

When planning your woodworking project, the cost of materials can be the determining factor. The cost of materials can range from 10 to 30 percent of the total cost. This cost includes labor, materials, and overhead costs, as well as time spent shopping, choosing boards, loading and unloading equipment, and storing materials. If you are planning to hire a woodworker, make sure to factor in the cost of materials plus their hourly rate.

You can find a variety of projects in plans and examples of woodworking online. Many of them don't require a lot of time or materials. Instead, you can use less expensive items and build them together with your family. For example, you can make a simple tool box to hold gardening supplies or a flower box. Another example is a solid step stool, which you can build in an hour. These are sturdy enough to be used by adults and children alike. You can even gift them as decorative items.

If you want to get started with woodworking, you can choose from hundreds of plans and examples of woodworking projects. These plans are designed for novices and experienced woodworkers alike. They include step-by-step instructions, a materials list, and full plans. Some of these plans are even designed to be beginner-friendly, so high school students can try them out.

Printed in Great Britain
by Amazon

27740059R00077